DUNDEE GREATS

Craig Brown

DUNDEE GREATS

Jim Hendry

Foreword by
Craig Brown
Assistant National Coach, S.F.A.

SPORTSPRINT PUBLISHING
EDINBURGH

ISBN 0 85976 347 1

Reprinted 1992

British Library Cataloguing in Publication Data

A catalogue record for this book is available from the British Library.

Phototypeset by Beecee Typesetting Services
Printed and bound in Great Britain by J. W. Arrowsmith Ltd., Bristol

Foreword

Whenever a Dundee player was becoming bombastic or, as they say in football language, getting 'Ba' heidit', the great Bob Shankly used to bring him back to earth with the timely reminder, 'We've all seen you play!'

Well, I am indeed fortunate that, although I have not seen all ten immortals in this excellent book actually play for the Club, I have personal, and first-hand knowledge of all but one, Billy Steel. Indeed, I have played with six of the men written about in such perceptive and poignant terms by author, Jim Hendry. In my spell at Dens Park as the first player brought to the Club by Bob Shankly and the last to be transferred out during his reign as Manager, Dundee F.C. had the best period of its illustrious history. It is not surprising, then, that Alex Hamilton, that most irrepressible character and brilliant full-back, Ian Ure, the rugged, blond centre half; and Alan Gilzean of the cultured cranium and lethal shot, figure so prominently in the text.

Bill Brown had just left the Club for Spurs and Doug Cowie was doing a truly magnificent job bringing on youngsters in the reserve team when I arrived in 1960. What a privilege it was to play at full back behind the ageing maestro, Cowie, whose control and passing were of the highest class. At that time Tommy Gallacher was the leading sports writer for the *Courier* and his informed reports were respected as they were avidly read by the players. On rare occasions he was actually known to praise me, which does confirm that he was not infallible.

It was in the reserve team that I enjoyed at first hand the skills of

Jocky Scott, a youngster who had returned from Chelsea. Playing alongside him was a treat because he had such an insightful knowledge of the game, a key factor in the success he has achieved as a manager. Of course, Jocky had the enviable job of being Manager at Dens where he was justifiably highly respected by players and staff alike. I feel sure that Jocky will continue to enhance his reputation in his new job as Manager of Dunfermline.

Although I had departed from Dens Park before John Duncan arrived, I did play in some games against him when he was a fellow, but much younger, student at Jordanhill College. He was a fine striker and it was not surprising that he followed the Gilzean trail down south. His playing, and managerial careers, again, were a credit to the excellent formative years he spent on Tayside. More recently, Jim Duffy, adorned the Dark Blue with distinction. When he suffered his horrendous knee injury which looked like finishing his career, a benefit match was arranged, followed by a Testimonial Dinner. It was my pleasure to be invited to speak at his Dinner which, under-standably, was attended by many of the great Dundee players, past and present. Jim has made a truly remarkable comeback, which only a player of his courage would have attempted and, as I write, he is still a stalwart in the Partick Thistle defence. He certainly deserves this chance to extend his career.

Charlie Cooke is, arguably, the most skilful player ever to wear the Dundee colours. His intricate footwork was always a treat to watch, and it is gratifying to learn that he is involved in Coaching Clinics, especially in North America, where he is imparting the knowledge he obtained playing in Scotland, England and in the USA. He is a devotee of the Dutch teaching maestro, Weil Coerver, and is instrumental in the development of all that is good in our game among youngsters worldwide.

It is, I think, accurate to note that the ten DUNDEE GREATS have 125 International Caps among them. Had these men been playing today, I'm sure the total would have been much greater and, when one considers the calibre of many of the players not included in this select list, it confirms the quality of them we are to read of in Jim Hendry's impressive book. There is no goalkeeper included. It is safe to say that with the 10 outfield players comprising a team in Dark Blue there would be no need for a goalkeeper!

Craig Brown, BA., DPE.,
Assistant National Coach, S.F.A.

Contents

Acknowledgements

The author is grateful to the *Daily Record*, the *Dundee Courier* and *Evening Telegraph*, and to the players themselves for providing the illustrations. Also, sincere thanks to the players, for their kind co-operation and to all others whose assistance was very welcome.

Introduction

The first clue that it was to be no easy task choosing 10 Dundee Greats emerged when my regular travelling companions to see the Dark Blues play put their collective minds together and produced a list nearer 30 in number than 20. The puzzle reached problem proportions when one insisted — 'You must start with Sinky. You can't write a book on Dundee Greats without him in it!'

Now to explain to the uninitiated Sinky — or plain Eric Sinclair to the football world outwith the confines of Dens Park — was a mighty fine player. He was loved by all who followed the club for his commitment to the cause and his determination to give his all no matter what kind of trying circumstances were conspiring to make the watching of Dundee at play more of a cause for worry than wonder. Sinclair's status with the support is undiminished to this day and he only has to appear at a club function to get a spontaneous standing ovation. He is that kind of guy.

If the truth be told, and if the final selection for a place in the Dundee Hall of Fame was my exclusive responsibility, then Eric might well have found a peg there. For I can think of few others who drew a bond of togetherness between field of play and terracing. And if the choice was mine alone, other less illustrious names might have crept in — the type of boyhood heroes we've all had — men like Jim Steele, Alex Bryce, Carl

1

Bertelsen believe it or not, Bobby Wilson, Thomson Allan, Billy Pirie and, in more recent times, guys like Bobby Geddes, Bobby Glennie, Robert Connor and Rab Shannon.

But how can it be fair to allow one quirky individual to bear the burden of choice? The book concentrates on post war to present day but even at that, two of the players who made the Dens Park top ten were never seen by me — namely Billy Steel and Tommy Gallacher. But history and legend demanded their inclusion, indeed, the difficulty was who to leave out from that great side of the early 1950s and likewise the Championship Giants of 1961-62.

That solid full-back battler Bobby Cox would surely have found his way into this Hall of Fame but for the fact that three members of that dazzling championship outfit were already chosen.

Three out of 11 is a fair representation I believe, although I know Cox's omission will spark many a protest from all who saw him play.

As local heroes go, they don't come much bigger than Cox, and if I can find the courage, I will apologise to him from the heart if I am ever fortunate enough to meet him.

Whether you approve of the 10 greats chosen or whether you don't, I hope you get as much enjoyment out of reading their stories as I did out of writing them.

CHAPTER ONE

Tommy Gallacher

THE DAY TOMMY GALLACHER DECIDED TO SIGN on the dotted line for Dundee Football Club was to have a major impact on the Tayside soccr public for far longer than the normal career span of a mere football player.

In the short term, Gallacher was to emerge as a cultured and classy wing half — pre-eminent in a team built on foundations of quality and finesse which emerged from the dark days of the Second World War to the bright sunshine of a golden era of domestic glory.

But when his career came to a self-imposed premature close some 11 years later, the gifted Gallacher kept his mind trained on all things football. The man who they said could make a ball talk took up the critic's pen to become football writer with the *Courier and Advertiser*, the Dundee-based D.C. Thomson daily newspaper that serves up irresistible reading for fans from Cardenden to Crieff to Carnoustie . . . but above all for the avid soccer public in the City of Discovery itself.

So just how did the fates conspire to bring Gallacher — one time amateur and Army physical education instructor — to Dens Park in the first instance? Why did the Renfrewshire lad, son of the Celtic legend Patsy Gallacher, not follow his famous father to the green and white Paradise in the East End of Glasgow?

It's a fascinating story . . . with the aforementioned Patsy,

a formidable Commanding Officer of the Gordon High-
landers, and an unknown gentleman in a great, green overcoat,
all claiming vital supporting roles to the silky Gallacher
himself.

It goes almost without saying that when your dad is none
other than 'Peerless Patsy' or 'The Mighty Atom' as Gallacher
Snr was known, he is going to wield a considerable influence on
the football career of an offspring with a natural talent for the
great game.

But the influence that Patsy Gallacher attempted to exert
was exactly the opposite of what you would expect. Said
Tommy: 'My father just did not want any of his five sons to be
players. Having left school himself at the age of 14, he was a
great believer in the value of education and he was determined
that I would get my higher leaving certificates. Coming from a
working class family, that was always considered to be a
worthwhile goal.

'I knew that if I succeeded in giving my father what he
wanted he would be so happy. I had to please him first and
then think about being a footballer. And, right enough, he was
really chuffed when I got my highers.'

Young Gallacher in fact, seemed destined for the Priest-
hood when he was dispatched to board at St Joseph's College
in Dumfries. There, Tommy eventually chose chemistry in
preference to theological study and when he returned home to
Scotstoun for war work, the promise first shown with St Paul's
Whiteinch Boys' Guild shone like a beacon from within the
talented ranks of Linwood Thistle.

It was at that point proud Patsy realised that the soccer
bred in the Gallacher bones was very much alive and kicking in
his second oldest son.

There were a number of clubs after him, but Patsy insisted
that wherever Tommy went to play football, it would be strictly
on amateur terms. Falkirk, managed by Tully Craig, who had
played alongside Patsy, got in touch only to be told — 'Forget
it, he'll be going to Queen's Park.' The Spiders from Hampden

Oh gee what have I done . . . Tommy Gallacher's infamous own goal which settled the Scottish Cup replay against Rangers at Dens Park in February 1955. Keeper Bill Brown and Dundee defender Davie Gray watch in horror as Billy Simpson (front) and Sammy Cox of Rangers get ready to celebrate.

Park were strictly an amateur outfit — a tradition they proudly uphold to this day — and it was in their direction that young Gallacher was being pushed, gently but firmly.

Said Tommy: 'I remember playing three trial games for Queen's Park and after each one I was asked to sign. But I would tell them I would first of all have to speak to my father about it. You see, the only team I'd heard about was Celtic and of course my father had been a famous player at Parkhead. When my brother Willie was pursued and signed by Celtic manager Willie Maley, my father knew nothing about it until it was finalised. So he made up his mind that I would not be signing for Celtic and his reasoning for this was quite simple. He felt that comparisons would be made all the time and that could be hard for me to handle. I think this would have been absolutely correct . . . and not for the first time, my father was right.

'So I wasn't keen to sign for Queen's and this put me in a

terrible position. After the third trial, Hugh Logan of Queen's called me into his office. He said — "I suppose you'll be wanting to speak to your father first." When I nodded he added: "Well, I've already seen him and his message to you is this — don't dare come home until you've signed!" '

With that business taken care of, Gallacher Jnr's career was at last off the starting blocks and he wasn't long in letting family favourites Celtic know what they were missing. His first team debut was against the Bhoys at Hampden, Tommy and Jimmy Delaney scoring two apiece in the 2-2 draw.

'Queen's were in the First Division then and they were a great bunch of lads . . . really enthusiastic. But their approach to the game didn't really suit me as a player. It was a case of getting the ball up the park and everybody chasing it, then when we were defending, everybody chase back. But although there were one helluva lot of fine players at Hampden, there was not the kind of repose in the team that I was looking for.'

It was at this stage that Tommy Gallacher first learned that — in football parlance at least — the customer may not always be right. Explained Tommy: 'You know Hampden, if you get an 8000 crowd, which was about normal for Queen's in these days, you'd quite easily think there were only a couple of hundred in.

'Well, there was this guy who used to stand in the North Enclosure. He always stood at the same spot and I don't think I'll ever forget him. No matter the weather, he always wore this huge green overcoat and every time the ball even looked like coming near me he would roar at the top of his voice — "Get rid of it Gallacher, get rid of it." In many instances the ball hadn't even reached me and he wanted it booted up the park! His advice was like a red rag to a bull as my game was about bringing the ball down and keeping hold of it until I could stroke it to a team-mate. This guy's advice never left me — I never followed it but I never forgot it either.'

Gallacher had signed for Queen's Park in 1942 while his day job was in the labs at the Royal Ordnance establishment at

Ice and easy . . . A Scottish Cup-tie at snow-bound Tannadice and Gallacher ushers the ball to safety watched by United's Jimmy Reid and Dundee keeper Bobby Henderson.

Bishopton. This was a reserved occupation — thus avoiding military service — but Tommy was keen to try something different and within seven weeks of packing it in, his call-up papers were on the doormat.

And so the Army Game began, although when Gallacher joined the Highland Light Infantry in January, 1945, the end of World War Two was only months away. Nevertheless, up at the Gordon Barracks, Bridge of Don, Aberdeen, Commanding Officer, Colonel Jock McGregor was eagerly awaiting the arrival of his newest recruit. For Colonel Jock was a keen football fan and he'd heard all about the Gallacher lad.

During the War years, professionals in the service would regularly guest for clubs close to wherever they were stationed.

'When I went to Aberdeen, Dundee United wanted me to

play for them but the CO said no and instead I found myself turning out for Aberdeen near the end of the season. By the time the new season was about to start, Dundee manager George Anderson, a good friend of the Colonel, had been in touch. So when I asked "Where will I be playing this season Sir?" the CO simply replied — "You're going to Dundee". And of course that was the beginning of my relationship with the club.'

Unknown to the young P.E. instructor, Colonel McGregor was still to play one more ace card in Gallacher's career . . . but more of that later.

Despite his guest appearance at Dens Park, Gallacher, by this time looking for a professional contract, had not yet settled on his next move. And there were no shortage of clubs pestering him for his signature.

'I could have gone to Morton and in fact I actually signed for St. Mirren. That was an amazing story — unbelievable but true. The President of the Scottish League at that time was Willie Waters — a real gentleman — who was Chairman of St. Mirren. He was chasing me all over the place to try and persuade me to join up at Love Street and I recall one night he caught up with me and a cousin in Clydebank where we had gone on a cycle run.'

This gentleman of the game finally got his man that night — or so he thought. After getting Tommy's signature at last, he insisted in taking young Gallacher to his father's pub, the International Bar which Hitler's blitz on Clydebank had failed to obliterate by a matter of just inches.

'He wanted my father to hear the news so we went into the family department of the pub and Mr Waters, who knew my father well, said "Patsy, I've just signed your son." My father replied deadpan: "Oh have you, let's see the form then." And when my father had the forms in his hands he simply tore them up in front of his eyes: Goodbye St. Mirren.'

Later, the Gallachers went to the Black Country to see what Wolverhampton Wanderers manager, Ted Vizard, had to

Tommy Gallacher wears the Dark Blue with pride.

offer. Said Tommy: 'Because of English League regulations it would have been a very complicated process signing for them. They were going to give my father money, they were going to give the manager of my father's pub money, and they were going to give me money . . . all because the rules dictated that an amateur in his first year as a pro couldn't earn more than £7 a week.

'As you can gather it was all very involved but it didn't matter. When I was down there I saw the Wolves players training — there seemed to be about 100 of them and I remember thinking— "Oh, oh, this club's not for me. How am I going to get a game with all these lads about!" '

Gallacher's great pal from Hampden and the Army was Sammy Cox who went on to carve a great career with Rangers and Scotland. George Anderson had wanted both at Dens and when Cox signed for Rangers he felt let down and he made sure young Gallacher knew it. So Tommy thought his Dens Park chance had gone, but after Dundee's indifferent start to season 1947-48, George was back knocking at the door.

'When I agreed to join up at Dens, I knew what I was joining. I'd played for the club and seen their style — it was like night and day from Queen's Park. I actually signed for a lot less than I could have got elsewhere but I was delighted. The emphasis was always on playing the ball about . . . people like Reggie Smith and Gibby McKenzie. Gibby used to talk me through games. "Haud it son, haud it." Or "right son get into that space there" . . . absolutely brilliant to play with and advice that was just a little bit different from that offered by my big Hampden friend with the green overcoat!'

Gallacher's arrival at Dens Park coincided with their return to 'A' Division and many of the Dark Blue players, including McKenzie, Smith and Ancell, later to manage the club, were nearing the twilight of their careers. At that time Gallacher was an inside right but he was to stamp his class, quality and authority on Dens Park folklore wearing the No. 4 jersey at right half.

'We were to play Celtic at Parkhead and Reggie Smith called off with a boil on his leg. George Anderson was in a bit of a panic about who to play at wing half and before the match he talked to Colonel McGregor, who had come down to Glasgow for the match, about his problem.

What a let-off . . . Dundee defender Billy Craig (No. 3) gets the ball away with keeper Bill Brown floundering. Willie Woodburn is in close attendance with Dundee's Gallacher and Danny Malloy watching.

McGregor's advice was simply: 'Play Gallacher — I've seen him at wing half in the Army.' Well that was just bluff because I'd never played wing half before other than once at Dumfries when Alfie Boyd had been injured. Very soon I was settled in that position. Reggie Smith and Bobby Ancell continued to play for a while . . . Reggie wasn't too keen on running but he could surely use that ball, a really brilliant player.

'When you think that Reggie had been capped for England in 1938 while playing for Milwall, a Second Division club, as an amateur, that shows you what sort of player he was.'

There were glory days ahead for Smith too. After a spell as Dundee United manager he moved to Brockville and was the managerial mastermind behind their Scottish Cup triumph in 1957 with two ex-Dundee players in the team, George Merchant and Andy Irvine.

The Dundee reputation for good passing and silky soccer was well established and in season 1948-49 they should have won the League Championship only to throw away the title on the last game of the season at Brockville.

Dark Blue followers flocked to Brockville that day on April 30, 1949 but there was disaster to follow.

'George Anderson was in a terrible state with nerves and there is no doubt he affected the players. The popular story was that we were locked in the dressing room for over an hour. That's not quite true but he did lock us in. Although he was a great psychologist, that was one move that backfired.

'The funny thing about that match was that there seemed to be several members of the Falkirk team who wanted us to win that day — and take the title. We hit them with everything in the first half but we couldn't get the ball past their brilliant little goalkeeper George Nicol. He was invincible — and he even saved Alex Stott's penalty — an impossible save. I remember Falkirk's opening goal. Archie Aikman was in the box and he tried a shot. He totally sclaffed it, I think it came off his heel, but anyway, it trickled slowly into the net with Johnny Lynch diving the other way. I'm afraid that summed up the way that game went for us. We were all absolutely sick that day . . . Falkirk won 4-1 and Rangers beat Albion Rovers at Coatbridge by the same score, future Dens manager, the late Willie Thornton, grabbing a treble, to claim the flag by a single point.

'It was a very sad end to a tremendous season. When we came up to the First Division, we were rarely below fourth place and in that 1948-49 season, my opinion is that we were a far better team than the one a couple of years later when Billy Steel came. Quite a few of my team-mates felt likewise but it was only when Billy came that Dundee started to win things.'

The near miss that ended so sadly at Brockville, fuelled the know-alls who reckoned Dapper Dundee didn't have the killer instinct necessary to win prizes. But they were soon to eat their words.

For in 1951 Dundee lifted the Scottish League Cup —

Take that . . . Gallacher scores a cracker against Falkirk at Dens beating a little goalkeeper who was later to play a hero's role for the Dark Blues, Bert Slater. The Falkirk defender is Ian Rae.

beating Rangers 3-2 in a thrilling Hampden final watched by a huge crowd. 'By then we were playing so well it was on the cards and to be perfectly honest we could have beaten any team. There was a superb spirit about the team and so many fine players. Men like Doug Cowie, Alfie Boyd, Gerry Follon, Bill Brown who was just a young laddie then. The secret was the great blend we had — boys who could stroke the ball about, boys who could get stuck in and boys who could run all day.'

Tommy Gallacher, for those who never saw him play, fell quite comfortably into the category of those boys who could stroke the ball about. He knocked on the international door often enough but, apart from one League cap, he was never honoured by his country.

This injustice wasn't missed by the football writers of the day who would wax lyrical about his deft touch in a campaign to persuade the selectors to see sense.

It was once written after a particularly majestic display: 'Gosh, you could almost hear the ball talking — and it has a Dundee accent.' It was widely agreed that Gallacher, the man with the talking feet, a snooty stylist, was simply a cut above the rest.

But the selectors chose not to listen although he was given umpteen consolation prizes — being named in the International Reserve XI in days long before Andy Roxburgh's squad system was even dreamed of.

That Hampden victory over Rangers was the perfect stage for Tommy. 'We played really well that day and deserved to win. It looked good for us at 2-1 but Bill Brown blundered when big George Young hit a long free kick into the box and Willie Thornton took advantage to equalise. But then in the last minute, Alf Boyd headed home Billy Steel's free-kick and there was no way back for Rangers. The Ibrox men were the kingpins in these day and to beat them at Hampden was a bit special.'

Gallacher recalls his visits to Ibrox with relish. 'The fans always had a very special welcome for me — I can't think why! Sammy Cox and I were always the best of pals but the things he used to call me during a game. You just wouldn't believe them. Let me just say there was a bit of a religious edge to our clashes.

'I recall one game which was getting a little bit out of hand. I found myself on the ground and there were two or three players all around me — team-mates and Rangers players alike trying to get at the ball. Sammy was obviously a bit worried that I might get a kicking and he came dashing up shouting "Let him up, let him up." I was certainly pleased to see him that time.'

On another occasion Tommy crossed swords with an equally famous Celtic player — Charlie Tully. Said Tommy: 'I never had any fears about the physical side of the game — to be honest, I rather enjoyed it. My father always said it was important to look after yourself — more so him being on the small side. His advice was to retaliate first! I always believed that if someone got at me during a match it was up to me to get him back. I thought that only fair. But the only time I deliberately went out to hurt a bloke was once when we played Celtic at Dens Park.

'Charlie Tully was at outside left for Celtic and I dispossessed him and played the ball up the park. The next think I knew, there was Charlie kicking me on the back of the leg. I was furious so I chased him across the park to get my revenge and I took this winder at him. Fortunately he saw it coming and jumped clear but the referee didn't miss it. He was called Willie Brittle and he came from Clydebank — I knew him quite well. When he rushed over to ask me my name I said — "Don't be silly, you know my name." He said "Listen Tommy think yourself lucky I'm only going to book you. You should be going off. What's your name!" Charlie was another good friend of mine but it just shows you what can happen in the heat of the moment.'

But younger readers should forget any notion that Gallacher was a tough guy. His strengths were all on the ball although as he himself points out he could handle himself when the going got tough.

The Second League Cup Final in October, 1952 had less happy memories. Gallacher was dropped for the semi-final and when Dundee conquered Kilmarnock 2-0 at Hampden with a Bobby Flavell double, Tommy was playing with the reserves. 'I'd had a wee fall out with George Anderson over bonus payments during a close season tour of Turkey and I was still narked enough not to invite him to my wedding even though he was a good friend of my father, having played against him in goal for Aberdeen. I never liked playing for the reserves at any time but that was the worst. It is a bad memory for me.'

The Scottish Cup holds no great joy for Gallacher — he is long since remembered for the 'own goal' he scored for Rangers to give them a 1-0 win at Dens in February 1955 after a goal-less game at Ibrox. Recalled Tommy: 'It was a diving header which went in like a rocket. The ball was meant to go for a corner but instead it found the corner of the net. Had it been a bit nearer the centre of goal it would have stuck in Bill Brown's mouth — that's how fast it was going.'

When Dundee reached Hampden at play Motherwell on April 19, 1952 — the second of three national finals within 12 months — there was more torment in store.

'I won't forget that one until my dying day. We were clear favourites and we went down the park straight from the kick off and split the Motherwell defence wide open. But from only 10 yards out and with just the keeper to beat Johnny Pattillo miss-hit his shot past the post. We were the better team by far in the first half and could have been three or four goals up with any luck at all.

'Their full-back Willie Kilmarnock cleared off the line no less than three times with the keeper beaten. He later admitted to me that at least two of them had been over the line. We met at the golf at Rosemount, Blairgowrie and he confessed sheepishly: "Two of them were over the line Tommy". My approximate reply was that it was all vey well him telling me that now because they'd won 4-0 to lift the Cup . . . or words to that effect! That scoreline makes it look like a hiding but it definitely wasn't although in the end we were demoralised.'

Despite the hiding Dundee had bridged the gap — leaving the pack behind to become one of Scottish football's Big Teams and the man who played as big a part in that transformation as anyone was manager-director George Anderson.

'He was a very astute man . . . brilliant at how he could handle players. And yet, sometimes he was the exact opposite and you'd think he'd taken a brainstorm. Nevertheless, he was years ahead of his time football-wise. He was talking about British Leagues and European Cups in the 1940s. George, and the like of Harry Swan, the chairman of Hibs, they were really go-ahead types, who really thought about the game and where it was going.

'He would get on to me about holding the ball too much

Hampden heroes . . . The Dundee side which beat Rangers 3-2 to win the League Cup in 1951 — the first of three Hampden Cup Final appearances within 12 months. From left — Johnny Pattillo, Jack Cowan, Jimmy Toner, Gerry Follon (partly hidden), Billy Steel, Manager-director George Anderson, Alf Boyd with the cup, Tommy Gallacher, Doug Cowie, Bobby Flavell, George Christie, coach, Reggie Smith (partly hidden), Bill Brown and 12th man Gordon Frew.

and before every match, just as the teams were about to take the field, George would give our captain Alf Boyd the ball to take out. Then he'd get another ball and give it to me saying "That one's for you to play with Tommy."

'He had the habit of going round all the players in the dressing room and rolling up their sleeves before they ran out. He would do this to me week in week out but I would have the sleeves rolled down again before I was on the park. George liked the sleeves rolled up but I liked to hold onto the cuffs. He would never get on to a player at half-time if there was any chance at all that the player would react badly.

'For example myself — I was always pretty keyed up and nobody could get on to me because I was likely to flare up. Very often, George would get onto one player and everyone knew that what he was saying was actually meant for another. There was this understanding and by getting things sorted out this way George showed he was a real shrewd cookie.

'Long before teams were going to special training camps and the like, Dundee were doing this. We were the first club to have blazer and flannels and after training every day would all be taken down to the town to have lunch. And if we were training in the afternoon we would do the same for high tea. George Anderson thought big, acted big and he paid big. Dundee's wages in these days were commensurate with any other top club — including Rangers.'

Gallacher looks back with dismay at some of the training methods used in these days. 'I could be awkward if I thought training was too arduous. Reuben Bennett when he was trainer used to have us hopping all the way up the steps going down to the corner of Dens Road and Provost Road. We would hop on the right leg and then hop on the left and I'm afraid I just couldn't see the value of that for the game of football.

'I always thought a hard training session on a Friday was the most ridiculous thing — burning energy when we should all have been saving for it for the match on the following day. Every player was asked to do the same at training regardless of their build.

'There was this player Jimmy Toner — small and slightly made but a very good footballer nevertheless — but if he trained every day through the week, by the time Saturday came he had nothing left to give. Jimmy used to pretend he was injured to avoid training, it was the only way he could save his energy for the match.'

The beginning of the end for Gallacher came when Willie Thornton, who was manager by that time, insisted the player should try and turn the clock back and revert to his original position of inside forward.

'I warned him it had been years since I last played there and would be caught all the time. But after about four or five games I found myself beginning to get used to this different role again. Then I was dropped and that made my mind up it was time I was seeking pastures new.'

But after 11 years of sterling service, Dundee insisted they wanted a fee. The player thought he deserved a free and told the club he would pack in if they didn't grant him one.

Willie Thornton insisted Gallacher wouldn't quit because he loved the game too much . . . but he underestimated the player's determination. 'I was 34 and had a few seasons left in me. Falkirk and Dunfermline wanted me to sign and, in retrospect, I was definitely stupid cutting off my nose to spite my face. Football was my life.

'I had been doing a column for the *Courier* for about 18 months and when I quit Dens they offered me a full-time job. I would never have believed at that time I would be there for 29 years.'

Tommy Gallacher freely admits he's had the best of both worlds — first as a player and later as football correspondent. Today, he gets his kicks from tracing the progress of nephew Kevin, once with Dundee United and now attempting to reclaim his Scotland jersey by turning it on for Coventry City. Every Saturday, you'll find Tommy Gallacher at either Dens or Tannadice.

But one thing's for sure . . . you won't hear him roaring to a home defender — 'Get rid of it!'

CHAPTER TWO

Billy Steel

HE WAS THE GAZZA OF AN AGE GONE BY . . . AND as heroes go, George Best might have run him close for star billing. This little man, made in Scotland, as if from girders and with a brain that was to football what Einstein's was to the Theory of Relativity, could stand comparison — comfortably — with any of the game's Greats.

But instead of being 'daft as a brush' Billy Steel was sharp as a tack — he was a hero when there were many, an idol in an era long before soccer's money-making opportunists had dreamed up media-hype, photo opportunities and guest appearances.

The proof of his prowess was in the seeing and none who witnessed Billy Steel at play would contest his claim for fame. And if any did feel like putting up an argument, no matter how flimsy, they'd best beware. For Steel, the closest to a Soccer God that Dens Park has ever seen, thrived on a verbal set-to in exactly the same way that he could take on and humble the most gifted of foes on the field of play.

It was no secret that Steel was as sharp with his tongue as he was tricky on his toes. And it's true that most who shared a dressing room peg with the Great Little Man — whether it be at Morton, Derby County or Dundee — were at some time or other on the receiving end of a Steel-edged rollicking. His Dens Park team-mates back in the 1950s were no different and

Little Big Man . . . Billy Steel training at Dens Park.

although many spent a daunting 90 minutes parrying — or trying to ignore — his acid comments, they loved him just the same.

For better or worse, Billy Steel was light years ahead of his time. He played football in an age when most pros considered a good career would be one spent with the same club with some honours and maybe international recognition thrown in to enhance their standing in the community. There was a going rate for the job — they would rarely become rich men — but it was a steady job with greater rewards than more mundane occupations offered plus the added bonus of recognition and, if they were really lucky, stardom.

But that wasn't the way Billy Steel saw his career. He cottoned on at a very early age that his talent was in the extra special category and by the time he was in his late teens his target was to leave football with £25,000 in his bank account. Whether it panned out that way we'll never know, but Billy Steel enrichened the lives of all who saw him.

The lad with mischief written all over his face preferred life in the fast lane. He played hard, even from his very first recorded impact on football as an eight-year-old in the Stirling-shire village of Dunipace, the smaller 'half' of the Burgh of Denny and Dunipace well-known to Dundee to Glasgow road users before the age of the motorway — when a hard shoulder was a form of body contact often exchanged between goalkeepers and centre-forwards.

It was the local Gala Day and the Dunipace Primary School headmaster was one short approaching the football competition. Enter little Steel — 'let him play, he's daft about fitba,' said one of the parents. Three years too young, Steel was in and the rest, as they say, is history.

From that day on, wherever his football took him, the name Billy Steel was to the fore and it was with great sadness that football fans the length and breadth of Britain heard of his death in California in May, 1982, at the age of 59.

Steel had left his mark on football — there's no doubt

Grace, style, and an impish grin.

about that — and one measure of his stature in the game is that the record fee of £23,500 George Anderson paid on September 21, 1950 was not surpassed in Scottish terms for more than a decade until George McLean moved from St. Mirren to Rangers.

The teenage Steel's first step towards the big-time was when he was tracked by Bo'ness Cadora committee man Bobby Craig. He had been checking the progress of the boy wonder and when young Steel turned it on in a Juvenile Cup Final at Newtown Park in the West Lothian mining town, Craig and his committee men saw enough to convince them that this lad was extra special.

Cadora was a home-made club started by Johnny Andretti the proprietor of an ice-cream cafe used by many a budding young player as a social base in Bo'ness but by that time they were sufficiently organised to dispatch a delegation off to Dunipace to sign Steel.

The player himself once related his side of the story: 'When Bo'ness Cadora secretary Andrew Smart persuaded me to sign forms for his club he had a pen in one hand, a fiver in the other, and I was going my holidays. Now, if anyone said it was the money that made me sign I'd be terribly hurt but I must admit that vacation was one of the best I've had!'

It wasn't long before bigger clubs would start to pay attention when the name Billy Steel was being discussed. And Rangers, among others, were caught napping when Leicester City moved smartly to take the youngster south to join the Filbert Street ground staff. But his stay there was short lived — the Leicester manager was dismissed and no-one remembered to renew the young Scot's contract!

And so the 16-year-old joined his second senior side when he signed as an amateur for St. Mirren but his spell there didn't set the heather on fire and he had more downs than ups. Morton was Steel's next port of call and he signed as a full pro on his 17th birthday with £50 in his back pocket. Andrew Smart's fiver paled in comparison . . . and Billy felt like a million dollars!

But war meant Morton saw little of the wee man except when he was on leave from the Army and greater things beckoned after Billy's dazzling debut performance for Scotland in the 1-1 draw with England at Wembley in 1947. A month later with interest now intense, Steel starred for Great Britain against the Rest of Europe at Hampden. His Cappielow days were numbered and on June 4 that year Derby County paid a record £15,500 for his signature.

The little man with the world at his feet — and remember he was aiming for a healthy bank balance by the time he'd kicked his last ball — wasn't the easiest of men to satisfy. His demands were ahead of his time but Derby boss Stuart McMillan was determined to land him.

Steel asked for and got a house and a job outside football and the deal was done. Everything pointed to club and player having a long and happy association. But when Billy Steel was involved, things never quite worked out that way. He was slow to settle and the mantle of being Britain's costliest footballer was proving hard to bear.

And his relationship with his Baseball Ground team-mates was fragile to say the least. Ex-Dens Parker George Hill recalls being in Hull with Tommy Gallacher when they spotted a shop owned by Raich Carter, the legendary England player who was a team-mate of Steel's at Derby. 'We went into the shop to have a look around and Carter came out from behind the counter, spotted our club blazers and said "Dundee boys . . . how's that little b – – – – – – Steel getting on! Carter told us that Billy had been there half an hour and was writing books on how to play at inside forward. He'd also tried to tell Carter how to play and it was obvious the two of them just hadn't got on.'

While everything seemed to go Billy's way on the international scene and the caps piled high in his display cabinet, his situation at Derby was going from bad to worse. With his wife home-sick, Billy told Derby he'd live in Scotland and travel down only for games. Such was his prowess on the field of play they first of all agreed to this demand which would obviously be labelled unreasonable from any less-gifted performer.

But it was an arrangement that was destined for failure and the gulf between club and player widened. Then Billy pulled off another sensation — he called a press conference in Glasgow. This was an unprecedented step but Steel handled the situation with aplomb and had the football writers eating out of his hand. The exercise of course had the desired effect and by the time Billy's contract expired on July 30 there was much speculation over his next move.

Of course, Billy Steel wasn't the only football personality of these days who was reckoned to be ahead of his time. George Anderson, director-manager at Dens Park was another and his imagination began to build a picture of the great Billy Steel in the Dark Blue of Dundee.

His mind was made up when he asked centre-forward Johnny Pattillo, who doubled as Mr Anderson's chauffeur and handyman, what he thought of the prospect. Said Pattillo: 'It would be a treat to have him in our side. He's a smashing player and he'd do well at Dens.'

Things moved quickly after that and Anderson thought he'd landed Steel for a cool £18,000 after all parties had been involved in hours of talks. But Derby decided to hold out for more and the deal was off. Anderson was distraught and he didn't feel any happier when newspaper speculation linked Steel with his boyhood favourites, the mighty Glasgow Rangers. The whole scenario was like a modern-day soap opera and the speculation reached such a peak that Ibrox boss Bill Struth issued a statement saying that Steel would not be joining the Govan club. For a short while Anderson felt a bit better but then he heard great rivals Aberdeen were in the frame, and that was as much as he could cope with.

His next trip to Derby was carried out with an SAS level of secrecy and on his return it was Anderson's turn to take centre stage when he called a press conference of his own. 'Gentlemen, I want to introduce you to Billy Steel, ex-Derby County and now of Dundee.' For once, the soccer scribes were speechless . . . well, almost.

George Anderson was made up and the Scottish football public was enthusiastic . . . but it was nothing to the joy in and around Dundee. Anderson and the Dens fans knew they had a pretty good side — and now that Steel was there the feeling was abroad that the club would at last start winning things. And of course that is exactly the way it worked out.

But there is an interesting story behind his decision to come to Dundee and Steel revealed more of his remarkable character in a special article he wrote for the Dundee Supporters Club annual.

In this he revealed that it was the kindness of Anderson

Here we go . . . Boyd leads Dundee out to do battle with the mighty Rangers.

which lured him to Dens Park and an illustrious spell in a sparkling career.

Steel wrote: 'One of the luckiest days of my football career was a Sunday of all days and this particular Sunday I never even saw a football. The day I refer to was in 1950 when I stepped into a high-powered Snipe limousine in George Square, Glasgow and met a man attired with his usual characteristics of bow tie and bowler hat.

'No doubt all Dundee fans recognise that I refer to Mr George Anderson and if it had not been for him I would probably have been an Aberdeen player because that very morning I had spoken to Mr David Halliday of Aberdeen regarding signing for the Dons.

'The reason I chose Dundee was simply that I remembered Mr Anderson from his Aberdeen days when I played with the Army teams who visited Pittodrie and remembered his kindness on these occasions.

27

'One day in particular will always remain with me when I was up at reveille in Edinburgh, caught the ten o'clock for Aberdeen, rushed to Linksfield and took part in a five-a-side competition. Our five were Jimmy Carabine, Tommy Walker, Bobby Campbell, George Sutherland and myself, all Signals' men stationed in Edinburgh. After collecting the first prize of National Savings Certificates at five o'clock, we caught a train out of Aberdeen ten minutes later.

'This was accomplished with the aid of a taxi driver who had no respect for human life. Entering the platform we anticipated a miserable journey until Mr Anderson appeared and led us to a reserved compartment which contained two boxes, one filled with sandwiches and fruit, the other containing lemonade, and to Jimmy Carabine's delight, a plentiful supply of Guinness.

'The conversation for the next few miles centred around Mr Anderson and the boys agreed it was a halo he should wear instead of a bowler, because after an Army breakfast at 7.15, no lunch and playing football, we were all beginning to feel a wee bit peckish.

'Result was that I decided Dundee was the place for me. I've been around more than most and found that at Dens they have a grand bunch of players. Of course, it's easy to laugh when you're winning but the Dark Blues still manage a smile irrespective of the result.

'Many great players have played against or with me, such as Wilf Mannion, Raich Carter, Peter Doherty, Stanley Matthews, Tom Finney, Billy Wright, Jimmy Dickenson, Joe Mercer, Dennis Compton, but for all that Dundee has a small town spirit or clannishness which gives a player a feeling of having an interest instead of being just one of a very large number.

'However, for all that, I honestly wish I had joined Dundee some years earlier and experienced the thrill of sitting on top of a bus circling slowly round the City Square with a Cup being held aloft, knowing that the team has achieved something.

'I've had some great experiences since coming to the Jute City and to think it all started on a Sunday and the responsible articles were a bottle of pop and a few cheese and spam sandwiches.'

Steel hadn't long to wait to get his birl around the city centre with a trophy in his hand as the club claimed League Cup glory just 13 months after his arrival — their first trophy in 41 years. The win over Rangers was the first of three Hampden appearances within a 12-month period and when they defeated Kilmarnock 2-0 in the following season's Final Dundee became the first club ever to retain the League Cup. But in between the Scottish Cup Final against Motherwell ended in tears as the unfancied Fir Park outfit won 4-0. There is a theory in and around the city that a famed seer, a bygone prophet, predicted in 1910 that the Scottish Cup would never again be brought back to Dundee after it was displayed in an undertaker's shop window following Dundee's one and only triumph in that contest when they beat Clyde in a replay. Subsequent defeats for Dundee and more recently, six out of six losses for neighbours United, give that theory a credence it maybe doesn't deserve.

Steel's first appearance for the club was a day not to be forgotten. He was far from full fitness but a crowd of 34,000 — more than 10,000 up on the previous attendance — thronged the Dens terraces to watch Dundee beat Aberdeen 2-0 with Steel scoring the opener to a roar that almost flattened the Law, the volcanic landmark that stands guard over the stadium.

Games against Aberdeen were always a bit special — this was the North East derby before the rise of Dundee United and it had the George Anderson v Davie Halliday edge thrown in for good measure. Team-mate Tommy Gallacher recalls with relish one Ne'er Day clash at Dens dominated by a very 'relaxed' Billy Steel. 'It being that time of year, Billy had been out all night and really he hadn't much idea where he was. He was staying in the RB Hotel and I picked him up in Reform

Street to take him to the match. He was the worse for wear so I took him to his room and tidied him up a bit. Honestly, he was half gassed and he tore Aberdeen apart. I think George Anderson knew what was going on but he turned a blind eye. But what a performance, drunk or not, Billy was brilliant that day.'

A legendary foe of Steel's was Aberdeen's Chris Anderson who as director and then vice-chairman did so much to take the Dons to the heights before his untimely death. There were 41,000 at Dens for a Cup tie and the press were making much of the Anderson-Steel confrontation. Billy was unabashed: 'I'll beat him 10 different ways and then I'll think of another 10 ways after that.' True to his word, Steel inspired Dundee to a convincing win.

Apart from taunting opponents, Steel loved to talk football and Doug Cowie recalls another of the dressing-room discussions that were commonplace around Dens Park. Said Cowie: 'One day we were arguing about the number of Aberdonians like myself who were coming to Dundee and making them a reasonable team. Billy questioned this and asked for examples. Someone mentioned Johnny Pattillo by that time near the end of his career, and Billy shrugged his shoulders and said "He can play nane." What about George Christie asked another — and Billy gave the same dismissive answer. Then someone said "Well, what about Doug Cowie?" There was the slightest hesitation by Billy and he said "Aye, alright, he can play a wee bit!"

'I took that as a big compliment from Billy because he didn't want anyone to be better than he was. He was the type of player who could win a game for you in five minutes but I don't think we saw the best of him at Dens. We were really only seeing him in flashes and he was getting to the veteran stage for in these days when you got to about 30 everyone regarded you as a veteran. He must have been a great player with Derby County when he was younger because at Dens Park he did enough to show he was world class. He trained on his own and

Yes Prime Minister . . . Premier Clement Attlee is introduced to Billy Steel and his Scotland colleagues prior to the 1947 international against England at Wembley.

I don't think it was ever the hardest of training he did but it was a real pleasure to play with him.

'He was some boy to get on with but I think that was because he was an out and out perfectionist. But I liked him a lot. He was a great lad and not just because of that compliment he paid me.'

Another of these dressing room discussions involved winger George Hill, known affectionately to one and all as Pud. 'There was no malice on my part and I think Billy understood but one day we were sitting in the bath talking about the team and I said to him — "You know Billy, I honestly think we were a better team here before you came." My point was that Billy's individual streak meant that he always wanted the ball — that was my argument and it was by no means a criticism of him as a player. But Billy's reply was short and to the target . . . "What did you win before I came?" ' Game, set and match to Billy Steel.

Hill's memory of these bygone days is razor sharp as he recalls names, places, arguments and incidents.

'I just think he could have been a much better player. He was very strong, fearless and frightened of nobody. But he tried to make everything happen round about him and George Christie on the left wing. Sometimes I played on that side and I would try and do something a bit different whereas if Billy wanted it back George gave him it. Instead of opening the play out, he kept it out on that side and the right winger could be running about not getting a chance to do anything.

'Once he had an argument with right-back Gerry Follon at half time and Gerry accused him of playing the match on tramlines. He didn't switch it about enough — that was a big fault.

'I can't say I approved of the way he was on the park — that was Billy Steel and what caused that was beyond my understanding, what made him behave that way.

'I thought he did himself an injustice on the park. You only get the ball when you're supposed to get it and that's for your own good. But Billy wanted the ball at all times, and that wasn't good for him and it certainly wasn't good for the club either. Maybe everything, according to the way Billy saw it, had to go through him, but there were a lot of good players in the team apart from Billy Steel. The half-back line at that time was Gallacher, Cowie and Boyd and there wasn't a better one in Scotland. They could play and that's not forgetting the other lads.

'We were playing United in a Scottish Cup replay in 1951. We'd drawn 2-2 at Dens on the Saturday in front of 38,000 and the replay was on a Wednesday afternoon with 25,000 at Tannadice. I was outside right in the first half and Billy was inside left and George Christie was outside left. George had to take quite a bit from Billy for example . . . that's the last f – – – – – – pass you'll ever get from me. And he would tell his opponent "imagine having a winger like that" and that kind of thing rankles with me.'

Centre-forward Pattillo, a big canny Granite-built man took goals — and criticism in his stride. Said Hill: 'Once Johnny scored from Billy's pass and as we ran back Steel shouted sarcastically — "It took you a wee while to think about that one, Johnny." He'd scored but still Billy wasn't happy.'

Hill knew that the crowd worshipped Steel but Billy took nothing for granted. 'Billy once said to me: "Football players didn't have a friend in the crowd." But he had plenty. They loved him and he was a good lad and I liked him too. I often wondered if he criticised so much because deep down he had an inferiority complex.'

Still good friends with Hill is Tommy Gallacher and he also has mixed feelings about the Steel days at Dens. 'His reputation came before him. Everyone knew he was a nark, a real moaner but funnily enough when he first came to the club, his first three games, he never opened his yap. And then, in the fourth game, God Almighty that was him started and I think Alfie Boyd got the brunt of it that day.

'The thing that used to annoy me more than anything

about Billy was that he was such a gifted player, if he'd encouraged some of the lads in the team instead of destroying them, I'm certain they would have played out of their skins. The first time he started on me I told him to shut up and get on with the game but Billy wouldn't let go. I was furious because I was quite exciteable as a player and when the half-time whistle went I ran ahead to the dressing room to wait for Billy. My firm intention was to plant him but Johnny Lynch took me aside and told me "You're wasting your time Tam. Regardless of what you do and what you say, you'll get the blame." And that was absolutely right because George Anderson had to stand by his big-money buy.

'But I don't think Billy ever realised the effect his moaning had on some of the younger lads. Guys like Albert Henderson who would work like a slave going up and down the park — Steely used to give him dog's abuse. I often wondered what affect Billy would have had on these lads if it had been encouragement but, sadly, he didn't seem to have that in him.

'But what skill he had, and the Dundee public worshipped the ground he walked on. I don't think I've ever known a hero as great as Billy Steel in all my time associated with Dundee. Any of the fans who saw him will tell you — "There will never be another like him."

'The things he could do with the ball. There was one trick he did and the first time I saw him perform it I called him all the lucky so-and-sos under the sun. He would take the ball up to an opponent, and hit it against their legs. In a way of reaction they would part their legs and Billy would stick the rebound between them and be off with the ball at his feet. I was wrong because Billy could do that time after time.

'Off the park you couldn't meet a better bloke. We used to meet him at DM Browns in the High Street on match days and by the time we got to Dens he'd have told us 50 jokes. It was a privilege to know him.'

His sense of humour was legendary and once a Glasgow newspaperman turned up at his doorstep in Renfrew to check out a rumour that Billy had been killed in a road accident.

Proud winners . . . the League Cup goes on show at Dens after the win over Rangers (Back — left to right) — Tommy Gallacher, Gerry Follon, Bill Brown, Doug Cowie, Jack Cowan. Middle — Johnny Pattillo, Directors Frank Graham, Bob Crighton, Andrew Clark, Jack Swaddell, Reggie Smith (trainer). Front — Jimmy Toner, Bobby Flavell, Jimmy Gellatly, Alfie Boyd, George Anderson (Manager-Director), Billy Steel and George Christie.

He was almost speechless as the Great Man himself answered the door and could barely get the words out . . . 'Billy! We'd heard you'd been killed in a smash.' 'Me,' said Steel, 'I've never been dead in my life!'

No-one was immune from Steel's barbed tongue but he always insisted his team-mates had every right to respond in kind. He once said to a distraught George Christie, his wing partner who was more liable than most to get a tongue-bashing: 'Look, George, don't worry about anything I say to you during the game. It's over and done with so just forget it.'

Christie knew that the bigger the game the louder Steel shouted and he was philosophical about the verbals that would inevitably come his way. Before a semi-final against Motherwell at Ibrox, Christie knew what he was in for saying:

'I'll need cotton wool in my ears today if I'm any judge.' He might have been wrong as Dundee romped to a 5-1 victory with Bobby Flavell grabbing a treble.

Even his international colleagues could be on the receiving end and Bobby Evans made headlines when he walked off during a match in Lisbon to warn the Scotland bench that something had to be done to curb Steel's comments.

A meeting was later called to clear the air and of course Steel was unmoved and he told his team-mates 'Once a player thinks he's good enough, that's when he starts slipping. A player should be his most severe critic. And if I make a mistake, go ahead and shout at me. Shout and criticise as much as you like. I won't object I can assure you.'

Despite his 30 caps, Steel seemed to have a love-hate relationship with Scotland's selectors and before one international they'd managed to make it clear that he was in grave danger of being dropped. Steel's answer was emphatic.

The seven wise men were at Parkhead to see Steel and his Dundee mates take on Celtic. Everyone knew Steel had to do something special to force the selectors to change their mind and pick him for the next Scotland game.

The game hadn't long started when Steel got hold of the ball and ran straight towards Celtic's right-half and his direct opponent Bobby Evans. Steel nutmegged him going up the park, turned and did it again going back towards his own goal and then, with the ball still tied to his toes, body-swerved two threatening defenders right out of the action.

That done, and with the huge crowd in awe at this display of cheeky individualism, Steel then hit a pass which Bobby Flavell only had to divert into the net.

Steel ran back to the centre circle with a smile of satisfaction staring directly at the selector's box. Not for him any modern-day gestures or signs . . . once again his feet had done the talking and yes, you've guessed, Billy was back in the Scotland team.

One of Steel's greatest moments came when he played for Great Britain against Europe at Hampden in 1947.

And on such a grand stage, it is no surprise that Billy pulled off something a bit special. It was described as one of the greatest goals Hampden has seen — he picked up a loose ball on the half way line, and tore through the middle taking Route One to goal. The Europe defenders weren't used to this kind of direct approach and they backed off, anticipating a pass, and refusing to commit themselves to a tackle.

Then, with Steel just 35 yards out, the defenders finally worked out what he was up to but it was too late and they could only watch as his long-range howitzer whizzed past into the net for a memorable goal.

That was Steel in his typical 'I'll show 'em' mood — the bigger they came, the harder they fell. He feared no-one and this was illustrated by his room-mate Willie Woodburn's experience before Scotland's famous 3-1 Wembley win in 1949.

It was one o'clock on the morning of the game, and Steel was sitting up in bed reading his favourite cowboy books and piling his cigarette doups high in his bedside ashtray. Woodburn pleaded with his team-mate that it was time for some shut-eye but Steel would have none of it saying — 'Don't worry Willie, it's only England we're playing in the morning.'

Another record-book entry in the Steel C.V. came in May 1951 when he became the first Scotland player to be sent off in a game that became known as the Battle of Vienna. Billy took umbrage when an Austrian flattened Scotland's man mountain George Young — one of Steel's best pals since they played together for Scotland Schoolboys. It was a tough and tousy game — all kinds of horrors being ignored by the match official — but all that changed when Steel perpetrated an innocuous misdemeanour in comparison to what had gone before and he was off. It was a chapter in Billy's career that he preferred not to talk about but the ref's decision was unjust in the extreme and the SFA obviously felt likewise as they took no disciplinary action against the player.

Fearless though he was on the park, the man they called Budgem in the Dens Park dressing room wasn't that tough in other circumstances. He would run a mile at the very mention of a dentist's chair and he'd emigrate at the prospect of being under the surgeon's knife. None who knew him were surprised that Steel simply wouldn't contemplate the simple operation he was assured would cure his on-going ankle problem.

He'd have four marvellous seasons at Dens Park — 131 League and Cup games in which he scored 46 goals — but his best days were behind him and, in typical Budgem fashion, when the end came there was nothing at all orthodox about it. Sure, Anderson and Steel went through protracted talks about his future, but preying on his mind was this dodgy ankle and the dawning truth that it was beginning to have a noticeable effect on his performances.

The perfectionist that he was, there was really only one solution for Steel and that was to quit soccer and head for the new life he'd always fancied in the United States of America. His mind was made up and there was nothing the genial Anderson could do to change it. It was the end of a Golden Era at Dens Park and who knows, perhaps Steel had even reached that magic £25,000 figure at the top of his bank balance. If so, he deserved every penny for Billy Steel was one in a million.

CHAPTER THREE

Doug Cowie

ALL WHO SAW DOUG COWIE IN THE DARK BLUE of Dundee and Scotland would be amazed to be told of the quiet Aberdonian's self-assessment in the early days of a blossoming football career.

For the youngster with the touch of an angel banished any thoughts or dreams of a pro career to the darkest recess of his imagination for the very simple reason that he didn't think he was good enough.

And even when Dundee's legendary manager-director George Anderson called at an Aberdeen shipyard to woo his signature, Cowie was still far from convinced . . . although he was flattered to be asked.

'That would have done me,' says Cowie in his gentle, thoughtful tone and an accent that today owes more to Dundee than his native Granite City. But his reluctance was anything but good enough for the bowler-hatted Anderson who sure knew a player when he saw one.

Fortunately for Dundee — and for that matter Scotland — George persisted and before the sun had set another sparkling gem was added to Anderson's Dens Park treasure chest.

Looking back, Cowie has a clear memory of the circumstances leading to his decision to go professional . . . and embark on a career at Dundee that would see him grace the World Cup Finals not once, but twice.

Representatives from Dundee and Aberdeen had seen the silky teenage craftsman playing at Gayfield in a benefit match, but there were no hints that things were about to happen quickly until after the match.

Said Doug: 'Dave Halliday, the manager of Aberdeen at the time came into the dressing room at the finish and asked me to sign. But I referred him to a Mr Mackie who was the secretary of St Clements Juniors and it was agreed that I would do nothing until training the following night. But as I was coming out of Gayfield this lad sidled up to me, asking where I worked, and telling me to do nothing until the boss had seen me. It was cloak and dagger stuff and I didn't know this lad from Adam.'

But the pieces of the puzzle came together the following morning as apprentice rivetter Cowie went about his duties at the John Lewis Shipyard when, in keeping with his modesty, all thoughts of signing for senior clubs had vanished from his mind.

Then, the mystery man from Gayfield the night before appeared at the quay looking for Cowie and there sitting in a car nearby was George Anderson. 'He came straight to the point and asked me — "How about signing for Dundee?" Well, to tell you the truth I didn't even know where Dundee was and I told Mr Anderson that I didn't think I was good enough, although it was nice to be asked. But Mr Anderson got my father who happened to be working across the road and my father said "If you promise to look after him, he can sign for Dundee."

'I was 19 then, I served my time as a rivetter before I came up to Dundee and since 1947 I've been a Dundonian.' Cowie won't be the last Aberdonian to refer to Dundee being 'up the road' but whatever way you look at it, Cowie was going 'up in the world'.

But he still had to be convinced he had the makings of a good pro. 'I always felt that professional footballers could do no wrong and that I would never ever be good enough. But it

Doug Cowie, class and
style were his
pedigree.

was only when I got into the game that I realised there were a lot of imperfections and that I could cope and hold my own.'

His first outing was against Brechin reserves and Dundee won 5-1. 'Mr Swaddell, one of the directors, always made a point of going to all the reserve matches, and while I felt there was a huge gulf between what I had been used to and playing Brechin he came up to me after the match and told me I'd played quite well. Now I thought I could have done an awful lot better but Mr Swaddell gave me that wee boost. I think the fact that I'd been spotted by George Anderson himself helped my career in these early stages and I became a regular in the reserves.

'I was still not confident in my ability but when I served my time and went to Dens Park full time I began to notice a lot of flaws even in training. Some of the lads who were regulars in the first team — passing a ball, trapping it, I could see some of them were not perfect after all. So I was beginning to think I might be just as good as these lads and that, too, helped my confidence.

'It took me a wee while to get into the first team and I didn't worry about that because I knew that the longer you dwelled in the reserves the more you would learn and when your chance came to step up you would be better equipped and more experienced to handle it.'

Cowie's big break came when Dundee went on tour to Italy, Germany and Austria in 1946 to take on British Army troops and provide some entertainment and relief for the soldiers who'd not long before liberated Europe from the Nazi threat.

And the call came when Cowie was least expecting it. 'We were due to play in Hamburg and centre half Tommy Gray was hurt before the match started. Now I wasn't even stripped and I had never played centre half and there were two or three experienced players standing by, men like Tommy Gallacher and Gerry Follon. But George Anderson told me to get stripped and get out there and in my haste I put on the wrong colour of shorts which for that reason if for no other made me a stand-out.'

The young Cowie did well and stayed in the side for the rest of the tour and at last began to believe that he could survive at this level . . . survive and perhaps even blossom to greater things.

Home on Scottish soil Cowie was back in the reserves to take his place in the queue for a first team jersey. 'There were plenty of good players holding down my position but it was then that I started to get a wee bit ambitious to take my career step by step . . . First I thought I could captain the reserves — it may not seem much nowadays — but then the captain had a big influence on the field of play. He could change things without any consultation with the bench which isn't the normal thing today.

'So I achieved that goal and that helped my development, as I had to use my judgement. I thought the next step was to make the first team and later I wanted to be captain. By the time that happened I knew I was good enough maybe even to play at a higher level and a Scotland cap would be my next target and I thought one day I might even captain Scotland.' More of that later.

By the time Dundee 'lost' the League in the last day of season 1948-49, Cowie was a settled first team man. 'I should never have played that game — I remember George Anderson sending me out all strapped up. At first the doctor thought my shoulder was dislocated but it wasn't and I went out all strapped up. It would be ridiculous playing like that today with all the physical contact there is but then you could take a wee chance. They maybe thought my skill will over-ride the injury — today you'd never get away with it, a chap with half your skill would run you to death.

'Our 4-1 defeat at Brockville to let Rangers win the League was a big disappointment but when I look back it was just kicking a football, a bit of fun. Although I always took my football seriously, I always hoped there was room for a wee bit of fun — it was a game and you were either no bad at it or no good at it.'

Cowie's breakthrough coincided with the emergence of Anderson's Dundee as one of the best sides in Scotland and their feat in reaching Hampden three times within 12 months — twice in the League Cup and once in the Scottish Cup — convinced the Dundee support that their team was on the move.

'I thought we were by far the better team against Rangers in 1951 in the first League Cup win but I must admit to being worried when they scored with just three minutes to go. The thought ran through my mind that Rangers never lost in extra time — that they were always the stronger side in these circumstances. But then Billy Steel chipped the ball on to Alfie Boyd's head and that was that — it was always great to beat Rangers but to do it at Hampen. . . . They were the team to beat in those days.

'The following year against Kilmarnock we didn't play anything like as well as we could have done. In fact they probably played better stuff than we did but Bobby Flavell snapped up two chances and we'd won again. I can possibly look back now and say the result was unfair on Killie but at the time we'd lifted the Cup and that was all that mattered. I always felt that the better team could lose a game but the best team won because the best team puts the ball in the back of the net. Killie felt hard done by and I must admit if Dundee had played their normal traditional good football — as Kilmarnock had done that day — and we'd lost 2-0, I would definitely have felt aggrieved.'

The Scottish Cup Final in between was no joyous occasion as Motherwell won 4-0 and Cowie's reflections suggest he would quite happily go out and play them again to seek a more satisfactory outcome. His words come out with some reluctance . . . 'a fiasco, I don't think there were four goals in it, we had three kicked off the line and some said they were behind the line, a sad, sad day for the club.'

Three of the best . . . A famous Dundee half-back line, Tommy Gallacher, Doug Cowie and Alfie Boyd.

That magic spell — two Hampden wins out of three — was the peak of George Anderson's achievements as a manager although Dundee Football Club should always be grateful for the manner in which he transformed them into the big time. And Doug Cowie, one of his best-ever signings, talks only in glowing terms.

'He looked after me like I was his son — I can't put it any other way, I think because he had spotted me at Arbroath and chased my signature — I think that gave him great pleasure and he saw me getting on in the world, getting into the first team and becoming an internationalist. I think he was a real purist. You could win games but he was the type who would be annoyed if you hadn't played good football in the process.

'George never had to tell you anything. If we hadn't played good football, he would just come in, take his bowler hat off, scratch his head, put his hat back on again and walk out of the dressing room. And we would all think ''Oh dear, the boss isn't happy at the way we're playing''. We might even

have been winning but he insisted on good football as well —
he was a real purist.'

'We would go to the likes of Pitlochry for a week's
training and it was nothing but the best. It was the Hydro for
Dundee, not some wee second rate joint away beyond the hills.
We went to South Africa in 1953 and when we came back that
great team was beginning to break up. We lost South Africans
Ken Zeising and Gordon Frew, Jack Cowan the Canadian left
back, we lost Alfie Boyd and we lost Billy Steel. You couldn't
buy these kind of players today. When Bobby Flavell went that
was the nucleus of a fine side and it was a case of having to
start all over again.

'Also I think maybe George Anderson thought he had
done all he could and that coupled with the loss of all these
players made it just too much of a job and so he passed it on to
Willie Thornton although we never really did much under
Willie because by that time the club was having to rebuild a
team again. By that time I was an internationalist and I felt a
wee bit of pressure being the only experienced man left.'

Thornton's coach Archie MacAuley, who had played for
Great Britain against the Rest of Europe while an Arsenal
player, brought new ideas — ideas that would have been alien
to George Anderson and ideas that were some distance from
the way Doug Cowie felt the game should be played.

'His method was that if the opposing team had the ball
deep in their own half, we were to retreat right back to our
18-yard line. I disagreed with that — and whether I should have
been outspoken or not — I argued with him. I asked why we
couldn't try to retrieve possession without having to give away
so much ground. I said when we got the ball back we would
have 80 yards to get it up the park and there would be a lot of
needless energy expended — everybody going up and back, up
and back but Archie couldn't see that.

'I got the feeling then as I do now that if you can't get a
team to go forward and attack I would rather come out of the
game altogether. But Archie didn't see it that way. Great player

Cowie's I.D. for the 1958 World Cup Finals in Sweden.

though he was I got the feeling that Archie just felt we weren't good enough to play football they way he'd always done it. It was as if he was saying — "I could do it in my day but I'm no happy with you boys doing it so I want you to go back and defend." '

This was a source of frustration for Cowie because George Anderson had encouraged him to play the attacking centre half game on tour — a ploy borne out of Anderson's dislike for the ultra-defensive stopper-type centre half. 'He thought in those days that the centre half was too defensive and so you can imagine what he would have thought of football now when you sometimes get three centre halves playing together, or two plus a sweeper!

'One day there was a Dundee-Dundee United select v Brechin, Arbroath and Forfar select in a benefit match and I asked Willie if I could try the attacking centre half game. He was happy to go along with that because there was nothing at stake. The way it worked was when the centre half went up the park, one of the wing halves would sit in and cover that area.

'Of course no-one knew what was happening and I was getting the whole field to myself — it worked a treat. Then I wanted to try it again and although Willie agreed, Archie said that he wanted it modified and I just wasn't happy to have it tampered with . . . I was seeing the game as I saw it out on the field and Archie was seeing it from the touchline.

'He got his way but modified, it just didn't work as well. I think Archie just wanted to have his finger in the pie as if he was trying to develop the tactics.

'That was the big difference between the George Anderson days and the Thornton-MacAuley regime. With George you attacked all the time, played good football, going forward and playing attacking, fluid football. With Willie Thornton came the Rangers idea of that time which was built on the Iron Curtain type defence. The inside men were not to go further up than the three front men, that is the two wingers and the centre forward, and at shies we were not to throw the ball back the way even if a defender was in oceans of space.

'We went to Brockville one day and we were leading 5-1 and Willie Thornton was shouting at us to hit the corner flag. After the game I said "Boss, what were you talking about hitting the corner flag?" and he said he wanted us to get the ball into the corners of the field and make them turn. I said that the corner flag wasn't wearing a Dark Blue shirt and when I pass the ball I want to hit a Dark Blue jersey. But that was Willie's idea of the game — I'm not saying he was not a good manager you understand, but that was his idea of how the game should be played and from then we went back and back and became a defensive team.'

As time marched on Cowie could see the gradual change in Dundee and he could see the beginning of the end of his days as a stalwart with the club.

'I was essentially an attacking wing half although I could do the job defensively as well because I'd been a centre half for years as well. We worked out a system at Dens using four half backs with a wee boy called Davie Sneddon from Kilmarnock.

Close call . . . Left back Jack Cowan clears the danger in the 1952 League Cup Final with grounded Ranger Willie Thornton and Dundee keeper Bill Brown helpless. Tommy Gallacher and Doug Cowie also keep a close watch.

When I attacked, Davie would fall back into the left half position and when Albert Henderson at right half moved up the park Davie Sneddon would do a similar covering job at that side of the park. Sneddon was a good little player and we never worried about being out of position as long as we had the ball. Bert Henderson was a real work horse and he was always ready to cover — but Davie Sneddon was an ideal foil, a cute little player who could hold the ball and use it very well.'

There were two occasions when Cowie could have moved on from Dens before his eventual departure to Morton in 1961 . . . one would have been to his liking and the other which most certainly wasn't!

'One Thursday night Willie Thornton came up to my house with my boots under his arm and told me he wanted me

49

to play for Cardiff City on Saturday. I said "Play for Cardiff what do you mean?" He told me a transfer had been arranged but I was not in so much of a hurry. I said I would go down to Wales with him, have a look around the place to see what I thought but Willie insisted that they wanted me signed for that Saturday. But I refused to go there with that kind of stipulation and the next thing was Danny Malloy was away in my place. But the move happened so quickly that I never had the chance to tell Danny what they were prepared to pay me.

'I never had the chance to say "Look Danny, they've been after me and this is what they were going to give me!" I was more experienced than Danny so he probably didn't get as much as they were prepared to give me.'

The other 'move' came to the surface in rather unusual circumstances. Cowie was a great pal of George 'Corky' Young, the legendary Rangers centre half through international meetings and once, when Young was asked to open a shop in Montrose, he called in on his pals Cowie and Tommy Gallacher to see if they fancied a day out.

'After George had performed the opening ceremony of this shop, I was at the toilet and George appeared and asked me how I liked the thought of playing for Rangers. I said I would love to play for Rangers and asked him what it was all about. Corky told me he'd been told to ask me how I would feel about joining Rangers and he said he would report my response to the Ibrox management.

'When it came to the time for me to re-sign with Dundee I asked Willie Thornton about the Rangers interest and he denied there had been any. When I told him that I knew for certain they wanted me to go to Ibrox he insisted that there was no interest. Now I always tried to be a gentleman but I think on this occasion I maybe lost the rag. I said "Look boss, you have your house, your car, everything you have is through your playing for Rangers and you are stopping me from getting that." At that time I was living in a tenement and had no car and I told Willie he was not giving me the chance to get the things he'd got from football. Eventually he said the club couldn't afford to let me go anyway and that was that and I had to stand by that decision.

'I wouldn't go as far as to say it riled me — you never know how these things would have panned out — but I think I would have enjoyed playing for Rangers.'

Cowie's first World Cup adventure to Switzerland in 1954 developed into a nightmare with the ill-prepared Tartan Lads ending up at the wrong end of a 7-0 hiding by Uruguay. Their build-up involved a friendly in Finland where Cowie and Hibs inside forward Bobby Johnston almost found the high life their downfall at international level.

'At the stadium in Helsinki there is a giant tower and Bobby and I went up to see the view. Unfortunately we were stuck at the top due to a lift breakdown and only got to the dressing room 20 minutes before kick off. But that experience didn't affect our performances because Bobby and I both won man-of-the-match awards!

'When the World Cup got underway I would say we were unlucky to lose 1-0 against Austria and then came the Uruguay match. I don't know why but they were a wee bit anxious about playing us but once they went three ahead they started to turn it on. It was a scorching hot day and we wore thick jerseys so by time up we were well beat and our tongues were hanging out. Manager Andy Beattie had resigned before the match and I don't suppose that helped.'

The 1958 event didn't really improve things for Scotland. 'We lost 3-2 to Paraguay at Norrkoping and yet drew with Yugoslavia who were quite highly rated.' Cowie didn't strip for the third game against France — we lost 2-1, and just like Switzerland in 1954, the Scots were wooden spoonists holding up the section. But we were making progress for this time we'd managed four goals and a single point!

Every player will confess to having a dream game at some stage in his career — a game when nothing went wrong and everything went right. For Doug Cowie that happened in the

Prater Stadium, Vienna in 1955 when Scotland thrashed Austria 4-1.

'Like everything else, your best memories are of the best games and mine came when Scotland went on tour to Yugoslavia, Austria and Hungary. They were all cracking teams and remember this was the time when Hungary had not long shattered England 6-3 at Wembley and 7-1 in Budapest with Ference Puskas, Nandor Hidegkuti and all . . . and the Slavs had beaten England 5-0 in Belgrade. Our first game was against Yugslavia and we drew 2-2, a great result although my job that scorching hot day was to sit on the bench and throw orange slices to the players on the field.

'But I was back in for the Austria game and we scored right from the kick off — Gordon Smith crossed and Archie Robertson slipped it into the back of the net. The Austrians hadn't even had a touch and they were a goal down. Naturally, that put our tails up and I thought we played super football that day and I felt personally that I couldn't play any better. We won 4-1, Gordon Smith scored the second, Liverpool's Billy Liddell got the third and it was last minute Lawrie Reilly to make it four.'

The Austrian game was a test of nerve as only four years earlier Scotland had been thrashed 4-1 and Billy Steel was sent off — the first Scot to make an early exit from an international. And there were moments when things looked quite ugly for the Scots, notably when one of the Austrians was sent off for flattening Gordon Smith for the umpteenth time.

'Lawrie Reilly had run over to remonstrate with the player before the ref dismissed him and some of the crowd came on to the park. One of the Austrian fans had a kick at Gordon and Lawrie just flattened him. That was the end of the aggro as the police moved in to finish the tidying up job Lawrie had started so emphatically.'

The Scots had to wait a week before they could get in and about the Hungarians who were beaing acclaimed kings of world football despite the fact that they'd tossed away their

Ouch . . . the home goalkeeper takes the weight of Cowie's challenge in a South African tour game in Durban.

chance the year before when an inferior West German side beat them in the World Cup Final in Berne.

'There was controversy in the papers about who would captain Scotland at the Nep Stadium and my name was being mentioned. Before that match we played a local side up in the mountains and in the dressing room Sir George Graham threw the ball to me. It was the only time I captained Scotland and even although it was only a warm-up game our pride was at stake and again we functioned very well and recorded a 6-0 victory. So in some way I did achieve my ultimate aim in football — my final target — to captain my country.

'I thought I had a chance of keeping the captaincy against Hungary but it was not to be — Gordon Smith got that honour. My first memory of the Hungary match was going out onto the track and seeing Ference Puskas striding up and down as if he was the best player in the world — mind you he wasn't far away — and I remember thinking he looked a real proud lad, so full of confidence.'

This was, in fact, one of the Galloping Major's last games for the Magyars as the 1956 troubles saw Puskas flee his native land to live in exile in Spain. Gordon Smith shocked the 100,000 crowd but a tactical switch at half time saved the day for the home nation.

'They had a big lad, Politis at centre and Hidegkuti, who normally functioned there, on the wing. But they switched it and Hidegkuti, a deep-lying centre forward, flummoxed us and we lost 3-1. Mind you we hit the post and the bar and Billy Liddell missed a penalty. So these Hungarians knew then that little Scotland could play football. My biggest regret in international football was that I wasn't able to play to the same peak as I had done against Austria. My strategy was always play the best you can and you'll help the team. We could just as easily have won that game and the crowd knew it — they cheered us off at the end.'

Like all Scots, Cowie was desperate to grace Wembley's hallowed turf and what a place to win his first cap. 'I'd been playing really well in matches for the Scottish League particularly against the English League at Ibrox — and that was very nearly the England team — and I thought if I didn't get picked for Scotland then I wasn't going to worry about it because I'd seen blokes playing a lot worse and still getting caps. Anyway, I was in and it was a great experience and a very good game, last minute Reilly doing it again for us with the equaliser in a 2-2 draw.'

The end came for Cowie when he was put on the transfer list by Bob Shankly in April 1961 and later freed. And sadly there was acrimony in the parting of the ways when Cowie, by then a Morton player, was told he couldn't train with the full-timers at Dens. 'Whether Bob saw me as the last of the Anderson men about the place and maybe felt I had too much influence I don't know. But it was a blow not being allowed to train at Dens. I got over it years and years ago but at the time I just couldn't understand why they should throw me out like that. I would have been quite happy with an explanation but I never really got one.'

After a happy spell at Morton when Cowie's brand of pure football brought the crowds flocking back to Cappielow, then a Second Division venue, Cowie had a crack at management with Raith Rovers.

But one incident gave him a clue that maybe he wasn't cut out for that role in football. 'I remember Albert Henderson, a great friend of mine, was manager of Arbroath and he brought his side to Stark's Park. They had a trialist on that day — a lad called Donnelly and he played really, really well. I was beginning to think in terms of getting the lad a trial for Raith when Albert came in at the end of the game and asked if I had a spare signing-on form. I knew right away it was for Donnelly and I thought — just for a second — I could say no and maybe have a word with the lad and maybe get him a trial. That might give me a 50-50 chance of landing him. But that just wasn't in me — I couldn't do anything like that and so Albert got his form and the player went on to have a good career with Arbroath.

'That was my first inkling that a manager maybe had to be a bit underhand to get what he wants but that would have gone against the grain with me and I'll tell you, if the situation had been reversed and I'd been looking for a form from Albert, he'd have given me it just the same.'

Cowie is happy to remain involved in soccer by scouting for Jim McLean and he's been the man responsible for many of the top class youngsters from in and around Dundee going to Tannadice — and if you knew the man at all you wouldn't be surprised to hear him call this the best job in the game.

And given his lack of self-belief at the outset of his career you wouldn't be surprised either at his conclusion as he looks back. 'I wouldn't have changed a thing . . . except that I would have tried to be a better player.' Relax Doug, you were good enough.

CHAPTER FOUR

Alex Hamilton

WHEN THE MAKER OF GREAT FOOTBALL players was dispensing modesty and all things circumspect, Alex Hamilton was at the front of the queue for the snappiest crewcut in town.

That was all Hammy required to complement a great line in patter and a dazzling smile that would put an acceptable and popular face on an overwhelming soccer self-confidence.

The Dens Park fans, who watched in admiration as the Dark Blues conquered Scotland's best on their way to the 1961-62 League Championship had fallen in love with Hammy's haircut, the impish grin and the abundance of skill that made him the player he was.

For Alex Hamilton was extra special and he knew it. And when Dundee's magical mix of silk and science took Europe by storm in the unforgettable European Cup campaign that followed, the bold Hammy was only too pleased to let the Continentals in on the secret.

To put it bluntly, there was no room for modesty in the Hamilton armoury as the cultivated right-back with the GI haircut went about writing his name in Scottish football's hall of fame.

'Any spare comps?' would be the cry from the 'away' dressing room whenever Dundee travelled. It all but drove manager Bob Shankly to distraction. 'Not you again Hammy,'

Shankly would say. 'You're always looking for tickets.' Then came the rapid-fire riposte — 'Well boss, it's me they're coming to see.'

A glance at the quality and class sharing a peg with Hamilton in that dressing room would have you wondering at the merits of his claim. But then, a look at that mischievous grin would give Hammy's game away, and you'd be hooked.

Such was the impact that famous Dundee team had on Scottish football, fans of opposing clubs could reel off the names ALMOST as rapidly as the Dark Blue suporters themselves.

Liney, Hamilton, Cox, Seith, Ure, Wishart, Smith, Penman, Cousin, Gilzean and Robertson.

The names trip off the tongue as easily as sardines on toast, bacon and eggs or whatever your choice. But in a culinary comparison, this was no corner cafe outfit. These names spelled out the class, quality and good taste only to be found at the best restaurant in town.

This was the team the popular former Scotsport presenter Arthur Montford described as the best club side ever to come out of Scottish football.

That's a bit of a bold assertion, but Arthur knows his football and he certainly wouldn't find any dissenting voices in the big crowds that thronged Dens Park to watch these men play.

Alex Hamilton, still chirping, still strutting, as he goes about his duties on the Dens Park commercial staff, is well-placed to add his testimonial.

Said Hammy: 'We were a match for anyone. The nucleus of an outstanding side had been at Dens Park for a year or two but the boss, Bob Shankly, played two or three master strokes which transformed us.

'The guy's knowledge of the game was incredible. And, God bless him, he never curtailed anyone into playing a basic system. Instead, he preferred good players doing it off the cuff. His signing of Bobby Seith, Bobby Wishart and Gordon Smith was inspirational. They were all guys who were a lot older than us but Shankly had obviously seen the vision and tactical stuff that we were capable of. By adding these three more mature players he was talking youth and experience in capital letters and these three wielded a very, very great influence on the side.

'It is an injection of a wee bit composure and a wee bit experience. And, clearly, he got it bang on because we ended up a very good side.'

It's obvious the affection Hamilton still has for the late Championship-winning boss — brother of Liverpool legend Bill — and he is happy to recall his qualities.

'He was an off-the-cuff kind of guy — he suited himself and avoided falling into the style and stereotype methods you would expect from a football manager. That rubbed off on the players because the guy at the top of the tree has a lot to do with the way people under him shape up.

'Trainer Sammy Kean was the perfect back-up for Bob — they put their ideas together — but at the end of the day Shankly was the man. He knew he was dealing with good players and he tried to conduct the traffic in their direction. But there was no curtailing where or how we were to go. He didn't have to blackboard us, and I'm sure the success we had stemmed from the respect he commanded from the players under him.'

Like many players before him — and no doubt many still to follow — Alexander William Hamilton was guided in the early part of his career by his father, Tom.

Although he was a slow starter at football — 'Yes, I played for my primary team but we only had 11 to pick from and I think I was the eleventh.' — Alex started to show some promise as a 15-year-old . . . boy against men in the hard school that was the local amateur league.

'The pitches were never great and there were a lot of hard players about so I would say my talent and skill were definitely stretched to the limit.

'I was asked down to Falkirk to train — former Dundee

On guard . . . Hamilton is ready for action at a corner kick.

player Reggie Smith was the manager at the time — but my dad said I was far too young to be getting involved with a club. Later, Rangers were interested in signing me but my dad knocked that in the head too. He wanted me to go to Dundee — he knew I'd get a chance there.'

But when Hamilton left secondary school in Fauldhouse, West Lothian, a career that was to grace Hampden, Wembley and many of Europe's finest stadiums, seemed an impossible dream.

His mother, Jean, bought Alex Hamilton an insurance book, and the young Hammy went out into the big bad world to earn his living. 'It was knock-on-the-door stuff and I did that right up until it was time to do my National Service in the Army. The Insurance game was my future at that stage and my boss used to say, "Well, lad, do well at this game and you can make a lot of money." But I knew I was heading for something more exciting.'

By now Hamilton was causing a stir with his performances for Westrigg Bluebell, a secondary juvenile outfit playing out of nearby Blackridge.

Talent scouts were a common sight round these parts, but the appearance at the village pitch of former Rangers and Scotland great Willie Thornton, then manager of Dundee, to see Hamilton for himself, had the place buzzing.

'That was a nightmare for me,' said Hammy. 'We were awarded a penalty and I was given the job of taking it. At the back of the ground is a slaughterhouse and that's what they had to do with the ball because that's where it ended up!'

But Thornton had seen enough and by the time Hamilton went into the Army his name was on provisional forms, stuck away in a safe corner of the manager's bottom drawer.

After being called up to the staff at the beginning of season 1957-58, Hamilton didn't have too long to wait for his chance. 'In these days the season began with League Cup sections and after a few games we found we couldn't qualify. The boss told me it was time I had a wee outing as he put it and

Keepy-uppy skill, from Alex Hamilton.

there I was playing against Ian Crawford of Hearts at Tynecastle. It was day and night from what I'd been used to and although we lost 4-2 I did reasonably well.

'Near the turn of the year Hugh Reid, the regular right back, was injured and the boss had no qualms about sticking me in. But in my first three games we lost 7-1 at Airdrie, 2-1 at

Dens against Aberdeen, 4-0 against Raith at Kirkcaldy and 5-0 at home to Hearts.

It was after that first match that Hamilton's Dens Park team-mates were beginning to get the measure of this cocky lad from Fauldhouse. Left back Bobby Cox, another immortal from the Championship and European Cup team was there when Hammy met up with his dad and uncle after that first match. Said Cox: 'I couldn't believe what I was hearing, we had just lost 7-1 and there was Hammy saying to his dad "After that performance I think I can get a game for Scotland." '

It's perhaps fitting that Cox — he of the famous sliding tackle — helps Hammy to entertain guests in the club's Billy Steel Lounge on match-days. Cox is smaller, and quieter by nature — enough to encourage Hamilton to wipe the floor with him once the repartee starts.

'Bobby keeps reminding me that he was skipper — and I'll just say "You? You couldn't captain a one-man rowing boat!" And I tell the punters there's a space on the boardroom wall next to my photograph and one of my caps. That's where Bobby is to be honoured . . . They're going to put up a pair of muddy shorts and a big divot from one of his tackles! Cox was never capped — rumour was it went to a vote at the selection committee meeting, but he lost out because they reckoned it would cost too much to returf Hampden once Bobby had finished with it.

'But seriously, Bobby was a far better back then he generally got credit for. Don't worry, the Dundee fans knew his value and the likes of Willie Henderson and Jimmy Johnstone never liked playing against him. Wingers thought they were away past him — then he'd flick that right peg into the sliding tackle and that would be that.'

With Hamilton established in the first team, it wasn't long before the young man who started working life knocking on doors for insurance money was knocking on the door for international recognition.

Juggling about . . . Hamilton has time to put on a show against Dundee United.

In 1961 he was chosen for the Scottish League against the Italian League — Denis Law, John Charles, Gerry Hitchin and all — and starred in a 1-1 draw at Hampden and Hamilton was on his way.

Quick off his mark and light on his feet, Hamilton didn't

particularly like tackling and wasn't the best in the air. But a winger who got the better of him was as rare as a Dundee United win at Hampden!

One who did, however, was little Joe McInnes of the long-lamented Third Lanark, who built a superb reputation as a footballing side in the early 1960s before their sad demise in 1967.

Hammy takes up the tale. 'The game hadn't long started and I could sense someone looking at me. It was Joe standing with hands on hips and he said "You don't even look like a fitba' player." At first I though he was speaking to someone else then the penny dropped — IT'S ME HE'S talking to. Then he said "When I get the ball at my feet pal, I'm going to turn you inside out." And believe me that's exactly what he did!

'You see, I was more intent in trying to nobble him than getting on with the game and he won our duel hands down.

'Afterwards, I sat down and thought about that episode and I thought about it long and hard. Here was a guy telling me how bad I was when I think I'm a good turn. I must try this to see if it'll work for me.

'Our next game against Thirds was at Cathkin and my direct opponent was a lad called Pat Buckley whose father Paddy was a star winger with Aberdeen. That day I'd asked the boss for a couple of extra complimentary tickets and took them on the park tucked into my shorts. The game hadn't long started when I said to the lad — you know I played against your old man. He must have thought we were in for a friendly wee blether but then I said — by the way, here's a couple of comps. When I sell you a wee dummy and you end up outside in the street, they'll get you back in!'

The Hammy dummy became a hallmark of his game — sometimes everyone in the ground could see it coming but he was so quick on his feet there was nothing his foe could do about it . . . except buy it on his way to a good old-fashioned chasing.

Hamilton was one of the first overlapping full backs in the

Scottish game and his philosophy was quite imaginative . . . better him chasing you than vice versa. And so attack became the best part of defence.

'I went forward at the first opportunity. My idea was to make the winger into a defensive player. It's all mental and it's all patter but allied to skill it works.'

The gift of pace obviously made that ploy a good bit easier to operate and that was an asset Hamilton had in abundance from a very early age.

'My dad reckoned it wasn't my strongest point and I recall how he used to keep pigeons — a very popular hobby in mining areas in these days. He would put a basket of doos on the back green and let them out. I had to try and catch them before they went five yards. I'm sure that grounding sharpened up my pace.

'Bob Shankly used to tell the story about the day he was sitting chatting to some journalists from down south who had come up for one of our European games at Dens. RAF Leuchars is just across the Tay from Dundee and there were lots of jets about making a roaring noise as they flew low over the park. One reporter said "My goodness, there are a few jets about today Mr Shankly." To which he replied "Jets? Nothing of the kind — it's just Hammy working on his sprints!" '

Wingers who did give Hamilton a headache included George Mulhall of Aberdeen and big John 'Yogi' Hughes of Celtic. 'John Hughes was very difficult to handle especially if he had the chance to run at you from a deep position. We always tried to pick him up early because he used to go all the way back and get the ball from the left back. Once he started running he was so difficult because he was such a big lad — because of his running power he could just brush you aside.

'Davy Wilson of Rangers was great to play against and the patter was brilliant. We'd have a carry on racing each other to the by-line. Sometime when I used to play Hughes I'd admit to getting a bit uptight because in the back of your mind you knew you could be in for a right hard time. I never looked at it like

that with Davy. One game he'd get the better of me, next time
it would be my turn, but there was never much in it. Patter-
wise, Davy would give as good as he got but I often wondered
what others thought when I was telling them how great I was
and how bad they were. Certainly, I know how I felt when Joe
McInnes outsmarted me that day — a right Wally I can tell
you.'

One of Hamilton's greatest claims to fame — and if
you've got the picture, they're queueing up to be heard — was
that he was never in a losing side against England, Bobby
Charlton and all.

'I played against them seven times — four full international and three League matches. Charlton was a very, very
good player — his record and reputation speak for themselves
— but I never ever worried about him. He always used to try
and get the ball onto his left peg — that was his strongest area
— I always tried to show him the line. He would throw himself
inside and then flick the ball to the outside. But I never
watched his feints and swerves. Bob Shankly always told me to
watch the ball saying "It's the ball you want to win, not the
man." Charlton was the classic reason for that advice — watch
him and you'd end up being sold a dummy and caught flat-
footed. I'd say to him — it's Hammy you're playing, I don't
buy dummies, I sell them!

'The first time I was against Charlton was when we played
the English League at Villa Park. I kicked the sole right off my
boot that night — not kicking him incidentally, that wasn't my
style — but it made no difference at all. I could have played in
my bare feet. Once at Hampden, Alf Ramsey was in the foyer
after the match looking for Charlton. One of the lads shouted
to him — "You'd best check our hamper, he might still be in
Hammy's back pocket."

'Another time I'd amuse the lads in our side during the
game by shouting: "Charlton, where's Charlton? I've no seen
him all day." These were great days.

'The first time I was at Wembley I was numb all the way

Watch it . . . Hamilton in action against Rangers at Ibrox.

from the hotel to the ground. No disrespect to Hampden, but I think it's every Scots lads dream to play at Wembley. When you're going up that road and you can see these two big towers and the place is absolutely seething with people . . . phew, what a feeling.

'It was just as well it's butterflies you get in your stomach — if it had been bees, I'd have a hive in there. Having beaten the English at Hampden as well as Wembley is magnificent.'

For Scotland fans there was nothing quite like a Wembley weekend so what was it like for the players after a 2-1 victory? 'I'd have to pass on that one, I'm afraid. Sure I felt great, but I didn't drink in these days and Jim Baxter, who'd scored both goals, persuaded me to have three or four bacardis with coke. I thought they tasted quite nice then suddenly it was lights out. I must be honest and say that after Baxter's hospitality it was a day out of my life. On the Sunday morning, I couldn't believe a man could be so under the weather.'

But despite that memory black-out, Hamilton can still fondly recall his Scotland experiences . . . great games, great players and great memories.

'Jim Baxter, Billy Bremner, Davy Wilson — they were all superb players and lovely people. Baxter once sat on the ball at Wembley as all fans like to recall. I didn't play on that occasion but *I* remember thinking "I've got confidence, but this guy — he's sitting on the ball at Wembley! What can his mind be made of."

'Paddy Crerand, Dave Mackay, John Greig — phenomenal to play with — all honest and good players. Crerand was the best striker of a ground pass that I've ever seen. He used to ping them, hit them on the drop and the ball would never rise an inch off the deck. I spent time with Paddy and he showed me how to do it. And Willie Henderson — he was great to play with — there was always an outlet when he was on the wing.

'I roomed with Eric Caldow — they always put the backs together and he told me before my first cap . . . "Play for

Alex leads Dundee on to the park.

yourself when you pull that Scotland jersey on — if you're doing your job that's all that matters.'' This was alien to me, the way we did things at Dens, but I quickly learned that his advice had merit. Eric's theory was simple — if 11 internationalists go out and do their job, there will be no problems. I think when you become a settled internationalist you might tend to become a bit selfish and wittingly or otherwise Eric's strategy might have something to do with it.'

Hamilton's 34 caps over five seasons was quite remarkable in an era when it was often charged that favour was shown to Old Firm players. Dundee director, former chairman and ex-president of the Scottish League, Ian Gellatly, sat for a number of years on the SFA International Committee and he's told Hamilton that if he'd been performing today, his portrait would be hanging proudly in the Hampden Hall of Fame, an honour reserved for all with 50 caps or more.

Hamilton exuded natural flair and talent but he wasn't afraid of hard work and practice to sharpen his game. 'I used to go back to Dens in the afternoon and try to land balls into a cardboard box about 30 or 40 yards away. I'd never get them in the box but with practice, I would get them all close. This worked a treat with a player like Alan Gilzean in the side. Gillie could win everything in the air for you and if he didn't score he could knock it down for Andy Penman, Alan Cousin or Bobby Wishart.

'Gillie knew that when I got 10 yards over that halfway line I would launch the ball into the target area. With the cardboard box we're talking about a sitting target. Gillie gave me a moving target running into space so these balls became very positive.'

It was a ploy used to stunning effect as Dundee surged into a massive lead at the top. But a series of bad results saw that margin vanish like snow off a dyke and suddenly Rangers were in poll position.

'We never panicked even though our fans were blowing a gasket. We knew we were good enough to get the flag and the game which finally turned the campaign our way was against St Mirren at Dens — on the Wednesday night before we were due at Muirton to play St Johnstone.

'It was our last home game of the season and there were 20,000 fans in to cheer us on. There was a bit of tension in our play but we went ahead when Alan Cousin scored in the first half. But then, horror of horrors, St Mirren were given a penalty. You could have heard a pin drop as Jim Clunie stepped forward to take the kick. He blasted it towards the postage stamp corner but suddenly there was an ear-splitting roar as Pat Liney flew across to touch it away.'

No Dark Blue fan of that era could possibly forget that night and with the crowd roaring on their heroes, Andy Penman scored a second to put the icing on the Dundee cake.

But there was more excitement still to come in a drama-packed night. For just 70 miles up the road at Pittodrie, Rangers were playing Aberdeen and the result there would be every bit as crucial in deciding this thrilling Championship race. Anything less than victory for the Ibrox men would swing the advantage back in favour of Dundee.

The ecstatic crowd shuffled slowly to the exits to the traditional but crackled strains of 'Up with the Bonnets of Bonnie Dundee' on the PA system. The fans knew word would soon come through from Pittodrie and the tension built agonisingly. As if to tease, the music stuttered two or three times, but still no announcement from Pittodrie.

Then finally, the announcer came on, obviously another victim of knee-wobbling tension. 'Attention please, attention please, here is the result from Pittodrie . . .' But, really, there was no need for him to say anything else — the emotion in his voice told the story and he was near to tears of delirious joy as he eventually blurted out that the Dons had won 1-0 to put the League Championship within touching distance of the Dark Blues. Nor for the first time that night the chilled, early-spring air was split by a huge roar.

That night 20,000 singing fans went home, their feet not touching the ground — knowing that a draw at least at Muirton on the Saturday, would give Dundee the title for the very first time.

The rest — as they say — is history and Dundee were heading for the European Cup. This was a great adventure but as Hamilton explains, it all might have turned out differently.

'This was the first time Bob Shankly thought about us playing system football. We drew FC Cologne in the first round and they were perhaps second or third favourites to win the trophy. As we began preparation for the first leg at Dens, Bob got us in the dressing room and told us we would be playing 4-2-4 against the Germans. This was a foreign statement to us because we'd never known anything of that kind before. We tried it out in bounce games on the Monday and Tuesday against the reserves and honest, it was a debacle. We were all worried sick by the Wednesday because that night we would be up against one of the best teams in Europe and we'd be using an untried system that had embarrassed us in practice.

'On the afternoon of the game Bob got us in the dressing room and said "Look, we've tried this new set-up for the last couple of days and obviously it's not going to work. So just get out there and play your normal game." ' That normal game was good enough for a stunning 8-1 victory that sent shock waves throughout Europe — and although Shankly's men eventually lost in the semi-final to AC Milan, it was an exciting adventure for one and all.

Hamilton, though, was disappointed. 'I saw the Final at Wembley between AC and Benfica and us playing badly could have beaten the pair of them.'

The look on his face gave the game away — for once in his life Alex Hamilton, ever-present in the Championship season, full back superb and character unsurpassed, was *NOT* kidding.

CHAPTER FIVE

Ian Ure

THE TALL, BLOND YOUNG MAN IN THE SMART
Dark Blue blazer could hardly believe his eyes. He sat in
the South Stand at Hampden Park and watched in awe at the
pace, control and array of tricks and magic from the silky
senors in the brilliant all-white strip.

It was a night of dazzling, debonair soccer that those
fortunate enough to be in the National Stadium on that night in
May 1960 would never forget.

The occasion was the European Cup Final between Real
Madrid and Eintracht Frankfurt, probably the greatest night
that proud Hampden has ever seen, a clash of one outstanding
team and another that might have been from another planet.
The 7-3 scoreline in favour of the Spaniards is carved in stone
in the memory bank of those present and the countless others
who watched on TV. By all who saw it, this was unanimously
labelled the greatest game ever played — and who could argue?

Certainly not the young Ure, part of the Dundee Football
Club party watching in admiration from the stand. For that
match was to change his life. It galvanised an honest club pro
into an internationalist, a laid-back hopeful with no real idea
of where his career was going into a dedicated, hard-working
perfectionist who would reach for the stars and catch a real
sparkler.

He watched at what the Spaniards could do with a ball and

took a good hard look at his career to date. Then, with the rapturous applause of an adoring Hampden crowd ringing in his ears, Ure made himself a promise. . . .

'You've just been playing at this game,' he told himself. 'From now on you're going to be a real player.'

And so the outing for the Dundee FC players that had started as a club jaunt at the close of another long, hard season, became a turning point for Ure.

Said Ure: 'Until I saw that match I didn't think I was ever going to break through to become a serious first division player. I just could not believe what I saw on the park that night, I had never seen anything like it before . . . the Spaniards, they must have come from another world. I saw incredible things. It started with the warm-up when I got the first clue that what we were about to witness was something extra special.

'I recall watching the full backs . . . one would kick the ball from the wrong side of his standing leg 50 yards to his partner who would kill it stone dead on his chest, knock it up, roll it over his shoulders, and hit the ball as it dropped to the ground right back to his partner's feet.

'Then came the game itself, the touch, the feel, the sheer artistry of it all — it was wonderful.

'That was definitely a watershed for me. I can remember Real taking the Cup around the Hampden track and the crowd rising in banks to applaud their performance. That's when I promised myself I was going to make something of my career. That next day I went back up to Dundee and I became a professional footballer.'

Ure had seen the future and the big, gangly Ayrshire laddie would never be the same again.

'From then on I started to practise, practise, practise. At that stage my ball control was dreadful but within a year I was in the Scottish team. I worked like a dog morning, noon and night. I would return to Dens Park in the afternoons, go into the small dressing room and get into wee, tight situations

Ian Ure, master of the game.

against the wall, kicking, controlling, heading, controlling, keeping the ball up. I once timed myself and managed to keep the ball up for three quarters of an hour and the sweat used to blind me. I must have touched the ball thousands of times and not once did it touch the ground.'

Ure's touch and control improved, and that was the only encouragement he needed.

'It was amazing, I was just another big, raw-boned laddie sort of playing at being a footballer. But from then on I really did become a pro and nobody worked harder at his trade. Had

I not seen that match, I don't honestly think I would have realised in time what was lacking from my game. It was ball control, pure and simple, and it made me quite a potent force, the fact that I could now receive the ball and control it that split second quicker and do something good with it that split second earlier.

'In my view, this is the difference between outstanding players and ordinary players — the ability to control the ball and move it on.'

The weeks and months went by as young Ure worked non-stop to improve his game. 'I kept working at control, control, control, I knew I was improving and could do things that a year earlier I would never have even tried. I had all the natural aggression in the world, all the attitude in the world and added to that the basic skills and ball control through hard work. Nothing else.'

Hard work never frightened Ian Francombe Ure, but as a young schoolboy in his native Ayr it seemed as if his energies might be channeled into the making of a top class rugby player. Ayr Academy encouraged only the oval ball and big Ure was a natural, using the athleticism and aggression which was to prove so vital in his soccer career with Dundee, Arsenal, Manchester United, St Mirren and Scotland.

'Rugby instilled in me a lot of the reputation I earned for being a hard tackler. The physical side of rugby really sharpened up my ability to tackle and get involved on a man-to-man level. One of my ambitions then was to play rugby for Scotland — I never seriously thought I'd make it as a footballer, although I had grown up as a football-mad wee lad from the age of five.

'We had a particularly good side at Ayr Academy and I think we went undefeated for three seasons.' Perhaps two of Ure's team-mates played no small part in that run — Rugby legend Ian 'Mighty Mouse' McLauchlan and Mike Denness, the Scot who went on to captain England at cricket.

Ure kept in touch with soccer, playing for Ayr Albion on Saturday afternoon's after turning out for the school rugger

Top man . . . Ure in action against England's Brian Douglas, watched by
(from left) John White, Jimmy Greaves and Dave Mackay.

team in the morning. 'Sure, it made me a wee bit tired, but it
also helped build up my stamina and attitude. My football
skills helped my rugby and vice versa and I believe that if I'd
continued to play rugby I would have reached the same height
as I did in football.'

To translate such bold talk into big-headedness would be
wrong. A more apt description would be a steely self-
confidence, and throughout his career Ian Ure had plenty of
that.

But still, even when he was performing well enough to play for the Scottish Association of Boys' Clubs, a career in football seemed unlikely. If anything, this sports mad young man who could turn his hand to cricket, football or rugby, and still look the part, seemed destined for Jordanhill College with a view to being a PE teacher. But then Dundee's Ayrshire scout Jimmy Ross came on the scene and persuaded Ure to hit the Road and the Miles to Dens Park.

'Jimmy said I could go up for a couple of weeks and get my digs paid for and all that. So off I went, just for a carry-on I thought, but I was thrown into pre-season training. Now, this was a bit of a shock. Although I was a fit young lad, I'd never trained seriously in my life, playing was my training, and here I was right in at the deep end with all Dundee's seasoned pros who, of course, had been through it all before.

'It was a bit of a shock, they were all running away from me and I didn't know where I was — but I just thought "Sod it, I can only do my best."

'At the end of the first week, I consequently learned that the manager Willie Thornton wanted to let me go back home. But apparently trainer Sammy Kean said to him you're making a mistake, keep this lad on, and I was asked to stay another week.

'Apparently Thornton didn't want me to sign after that either. But Sammy Kean made a case for me and that was that. I couldn't believe it, they offered me £100 signing on fee, at that time I didn't have 100 pennies. I had no idea what I really wanted and suddenly I am offered a contract as a professional footballer so I jumped at it, £100 seemed like £100,000 in those days.

'There were no negotiations. I really had no serious thoughts about being a professional footballer but I thought, I like doing this — I'll give it a go.'

From that point, Ure's destiny was still unclear — he broke through to the first team as understudy to Doug Cowie in the No. 6 jersey but the role was not for him. So when Bob

Champions . . . Champagne time in the Muirton dressing room after Dundee's 3-0 win over St Johnstone which clinched the title.

Shankly arrived to take over the manager's seat, Ure was very soon holding down the centre half spot as a career that had promised much for two or three years finally took off.

Said Ure: 'The moment Bob came through the door at Dens, he proved to be a revelation. At that time Dundee had a number of older players who were on their last legs and who didn't seem to be that keen any more on making any kind of impact.

'Bob spotted these guys right away and gave them free transfers, found them other clubs or generally just moved them on, before bringing in his own men.'

Ure is a member of the Bobby Seith-Bobby Wishart fan club, two of the three veterans introduced to apply the finishing touches to a side soon to win the League Crown. 'I became the kind of legs between these two. They were the old heads, the creative parts of the machine and I became the mobile one, the hit-man between them. But I will argue to this day that there was much more to my game than being a strong man. Centre halves then were mostly still out of the old mould — kicking or heading the ball as far up the park as possible. But once I'd become confident about my control and touch I would always be willing to pass the ball on and find position to be able to receive it. In these days it was a hairy kind of existence but I broke the mould and Bob Shankly encouraged me to do it.

Shankly brought the team together, fired all the chancers who were never going anywhere. It was when he arrived that things went on the up again. He was a very brusque, un-approachable man, unlike his brother Bill who was the opposite, yet they were made from the same mould if you like, honest as the day was long.

'He told you the truth, there was no double talk, in the dressing room. If you had a bad first half he got right to the point, he never failed to get the man who was not pulling his weight, never failed to come in and bollock the man who deserved to be bollocked.

'Unlike some, Bob would never target the youngster who had been trying like a bear and ignore the experienced guy who had maybe been hiding and not doing his bit. That was his attribute, that and his sheer honesty at a time when there was not too much honesty in football, his just shone through.

'I think that got through to the players so they started pulling for him, everyone was working for him.

'Sammy Kean was an old pro and a great influence, a good man to have about the place. A terrible trainer — there was nothing scientific about Sammy's training, but at the end of the day you were fit.

'I used to go to Sammy when I wanted something sorted out. I was getting caught on the ball and asked Sammy to help me. He told me, when you receive the ball just make a quick couple of yards motion — it is amazing how nobody will come

Ouch . . . Ure grimaces as the bandaged Bert Slater takes another mouthful of studs from a Cologne forward in Germany.

near you — and it worked. You could go to Sammy with all kinds of wee things.'

Ian Ure reckons that the season before the Championship was won, there were precious few clues that great things were around the corner. But the 1961-62 campaign had not long started before he began to suspect they might be into something special.

But the slump after the turn of the year, when Dundee treated the title like a greasy pole, threatened to bring all the hopes and dreams crumbling and Ure blames that on the fact that Dundee began to believe what they were reading in the papers.

'There is no doubt in my mind that the good grounds in the early part of the season suited our game to perfection. We definitely started to believe we were top notchers and the feeling about was that we would only have to coast through the rest of the season. Unfortunately, all these wee things got to us psychologically — you just try that wee half ounce less and before you know what's happening, things are slipping.

'Everyone had been saying it was a one-horse race, a cake-walk for Dundee. We began to believe that and paid the price. The result was that once we got our noses in front again, there would be no mistakes second time of asking.'

The games that stick out in Ure's memory were the 5-1 thrashing of Rangers in the Ibrox fog and the last game triumph at Muirton which clinched the flag and sentenced St Johnstone to Second Division football.

'The match at Ibrox showed Bob Shankly's tactical genius. Jim Baxter was the man who made Rangers tick and Bob put Andy Penman on him as a man marker. Now Andy was a lovely player, one of the most skilful I had ever seen, but he couldn't tackle a fish supper . . . and there was Bob telling him to deal with Baxter. Well, believe it or not, Bob's ploy worked a treat — Andy would just sit close to Baxter and somehow or other deny him the space he needed to work the ball. Andy was an out-and-out attacking player and he wouldn't chase back to save his life. But Andy never fell for any of Baxter's shimmies or dummies and that made all the difference.

'That was the day most of our fans missed out because it was very, very foggy and the rumour got out that the game was off and many of the buses turned back. I don't remember much about the game except that we seemed to score nearly every time we went up the park.

'My main memory was of the Muirton game — I will never forget that — it was a wonderful, wonderful day, but I don't remember too much to be honest about all the games leading up to it when we were making a push. I do remember scraping through a lot of games, we were battling, perhaps we would be a goal down but we would go right to the end and with the help of a few breaks here and there we would get the win. Maybe it was written up there somewhere that Dundee were going to win the Championship.

Eyes front . . . More action from Cologne, with stand-in keeper Andy Penman looking less than confident.

'Muirton was one of the greatest days of my life if not the greatest. I remember we were quite inebriated by the time we got back down that road to Dundee. We had a few half bottles up the back of the bus and by the time we got to the City Square, I was well pissed. We went into the Chairman's house overlooking the Tay, a lovely garden and we had a few bevvies. It was a beautiful night and of course it had been a beautiful day, it was a scorcher and it was just parties right through the night — it was some night. Undoubtedly, it was one of my best moments. Dundee had not won the league before, it was a great thing, especially the way they had done it, having a lead, surrendering it, and then coming back strongly at the finish. Everybody had written us off as a flash in the pan, a provincial side that were incapable of doing it for the whole season. They said we wouldn't stick the pace but we did even though we did it the hard way.'

The Championship won, the Dundee players went into their close-season break in that summer of 1962, knowing that a European Cup adventure lay round the corner, but none of them daring to hope for the Boy's Own stuff that was to follow.

But first, there was a summer tour to New York where Bob Shankly's men took on Hajduk Split, Palermo from Italy, FC America from Brazil, Guadalajara from Mexico and West German outfit Reutlingen. The Randall's Island tournament on a pitch littered with nuts and bolts and temperatures very nearly off the top of the thermometer, conspired to give Dundee an indifferent passage but it was experience that would prove priceless in Europe.

Said Ure: 'The New York thing was an eye-opener. They all had so much touch and skill, everything was done so slowly until they got to the box then they would tear you to bits with wall passes flying about at 200 miles an hour. It bewildered us at the time but it was one of the best things Shankly did — it was invaluable for what was to follow.'

Once Ure starts talking about the European adventure, his eyes light up and his chest billows with pride.

He talks in glowing terms of the team-work that made Dundee FC the talk of European football; the heroic individual performances, that put the Dark Blues just one step away from a Wembley Final. But he also remembers some hairy moments as the chapters unfolded.

'The return game in Cologne after we'd won 8-1 at Dens still mystifies me. I just don't know how we managed to hold out under the most intimidating circumstances you could imagine.

'Cologne won 4-0 and by half-time they must have been odds-on to win the tie. At the interval Bert Slater was lying in a coma on the treatment table and we had Andy Penman in goal. I don't know who nominated Andy as the man to take over after Bert had been kicked in the head, but whoever it was . . . well, let me just say that they've made more sensible decisions.

Andy was hopeless, totally useless, but fortunately he wasn't in for that long, as Bert returned early in the second half.

'How he managed to play I'll never know. He was concussed and to this day he can remember nothing about the intense pressure of that second half. But Bert was the toughest of the tough. We called him Punchy because he looked like a wee boxer, he had so many scars from kicks about the face, thick ears and the like but he was a hard, hard man. But that night he was a hero — his performance was unbelievable and I have never seen so many point-blank saves as Bert made that night.

'I must say that night was one of the few times I was disappointed in my team-mates. Half of them s – – – their knickers — they bottled it, lost all their shape and all their form. They just wanted to kick it up the park as hard as they could and consequently the Germans had us right back on our heels. All the attributes that made us so good against the Continentals were forgotten and everyone panicked. Bob Shankly was going berserk at half time but by then too many heads had been lost and our boys were running about like headless chickens and I'll tell you, we did well to hold on

'To be perfectly honest about it, I ran about that night trying to kick Germans. How I never got sent off I will never know. I deliberately ran about throwing the weight about — putting as many of these white shirts up in the air as I could.

'I really lost the head myself that night but I'll tell you I'm glad I did. Because if I hadn't . . . Bobby Cox, Bert Slater and myself, if we hadn't really got stuck into the Germans the whole thing would have folded — it could have been 10-0 for Cologne.

'It was terrible what happened to Bert Slater — he was a target right from the start and I remember when he came back on, his head wrapped in bandages, that didn't stop Cologne trying to catch him a second time. It was just deliberate provocation and I'm afraid we weren't up to it that night. Too many did it in their pants and didn't battle as hard as they should have done.'

Ure's comments about kicking Germans shouldn't take on any Basil Fawlty proportions. Their origin didn't matter — Ure hated their deliberate attempts to wound Slater, and he responded in the only way he felt fit. Had his granny been in a white shirt that night, she'd have done well to look over her shoulder.

Happily, Ure's pride in his team-mates was restored in subsequent rounds and most of his memories of these ties are fond ones.

'In the second round we played in Lisbon against Sporting and that was a perfect description of the game. A 1-0 defeat in Portugal was a great result for us because, frankly, they could have won better than that but I knew they wouldn't live with us at Dens and that's the way it turned out as we won 4-1. We destroyed them, I don't think any team could have come to Dundee in the European Cup and beaten us.

'That year, the best football we played was against Anderlecht in the quarter-final at the Heysel Stadium. We played classic football to win 4-1 and I recall at the end of the game the Belgian crowd — and there were more than 60,000 in that night, rose to a man and clapped us off. Anderlecht were a fine side but these fans knew that what they had seen was something very, very special. It was astonishing stuff from Dundee, our possession football that night was just incredible. We were papping the ball about on our own 18-yard box — inviting men into tackles and then moving the ball onto a team-mate, a touch here, a touch there with the Belgians unable to do anything about it.

'It was simply the best Dundee performance I was ever involved in. Yes, the Belgians clapped us off that night which in terms of European football is kind of unknown.'

The Anderlecht aces dispensed with — Dundee won the second leg 2-1 — and it was next stop San Siro to face the might of AC Milan, and Ure remembers this one as if it was yesterday.

'I remember at half-time in the semi-final at the San Siro

Three of the best . . . Bobby Seith, Ian Ure and Bobby Wishart, Dundee's brilliant half-back line.

in Milan, it was one each and I went for a pee and I remember suddenly the backs of my legs started trembling. It was 1-1 at half time and I knew the final was at Wembley, we had given as good as we received. The backs of my legs started knocking — I think it was a realisation that it was Wembley for the European Cup Final that awaited the winner.

'And believe me, no team in the world would have lived with Dundee at Wembley at that time, I have never been surer of anything in my life. No team in the world could have beaten us on that surface, so wonderful to play on. I had just played there with the Scottish team and it was like a bowling green. We would have swept Benfica aside because we had already taken care of the Portuguese champions Sporting Lisbon, we would have definitely beaten Benfica no doubt about it. Eusebio and all. But then of course, Milan caught us with two rapid goals, bang, bang, within 10 minutes early in the second half and it was gone. It was just deadly finishing, clinical Italian finishing, near-post flashing headers, quick front men nipping in, the kind of thing defenders could not do anything about.

'Okay, you could say defenders should have been able to cope, but they just hit us and got us on the rack and we allowed ourselves to be forced back a wee bit. In the first half we had taken the game to them. We thought there was no point in defending in depth as our style was to go forward and play possession football and it worked beautifully up until half-time.

'I don't subscribe to the skull-duggery theory about cameras flashing close to Bert Slater and although the papers made a big thing of this I don't think it had any bearing. It certainly did not put me off and I don't honestly think that was a valid excuse. Their clinical finishing was impressive when forwards lose their marker and get there first. Sometimes the keeper can save them, but that night there was nothing Bert could do and the tie was gone.

'But there again when we got them back at Dens we beat them 1-0 but it could have been 10-0 if the referee had been doing his job. After we had scored, Gordon Smith was felled in the penalty box by a deliberate right-hander — it should have been a penalty. The defender just downed him — bang! Everyone in the park saw it but the referee and the linesman.

'But we should have scored a lot of goals that night, we gave them a hiding. In fact they should have scored first — I made a ricket very early in the game and their centre forward Altafini went straight through the middle and at that time he was a bit deadly when it came to finishing, but he missed. I can't remember whether Bert made a great save or he hit the post or something but it was an open goal which should have spelt the end for us but he missed.

'We went down and scored, and after that we gave them a pounding, meanwhile they were kicking Gillie up and down, it was cynical, Italian cattenacio type defending. With half an ounce of luck we could have got the 5-1 back no problem.'

Prize guys . . . The men who brought the League flag to Dens Park. Back (from left): Andy Penman, Bobby Seith, Alex Stuart, Pat Liney, Bobby Wishart, Craig Brown, Bobby Waddell. Front: Gordon Smith, Alex Hamilton, Ian Ure, Bobby Cox, Alan Cousin, Alan Gilzean and Hugh Robertson.

By this time, Ure knew his Dens Park days were numbered. He had this burning ambition to stretch his talents to the absolute limit and for him that meant English football and — if possible Arsenal, a club he'd always though the best of the lot.

Ure had actually wanted to leave after the Championship season but he was persuaded by Shankly to give it one more year.

'I'm obviously very glad that I did stay because the European Cup was such a marvellous experience. But there was no way I was staying any longer. I threatened to go on the dole and all that kind of thing because in these days a player did not have any say in his destiny. But although I took part in the pre-season training with Dundee they realised there was little point in keeping me if I was so unhappy.

'I wanted to go to Arsenal and I was so chuffed when they came in for me. Although they were not doing well at the time and had not won anything for a good few years they were a truly great club. By my reckoning Arsenal are simply the best. I played for Manchester United as well but they just don't compare . . . Arsenal's tradition, the set-up, the ambience within the club. Everything was style and class and I am talking about lean years when I was at Highbury between 1963 and 1969. So I can imagine how great it must be to be about the place just now when they are winning League Championships.'

Ure's move to Old Trafford was an eye opener. 'I was quite shocked at the state of the club — they really were in a bad way. The team that had won the European Cup was past its best and I got the feeling people there were content to live on past glories. I was approaching 30 and the move was a chance to put a few quid in my pocket and I always said you had to cut a stick when you saw it. Not long after I left Arsenal, my knee was beginning to play up and looking back, I reckon I was playing under false pretences in the closing stages of my Manchester United career, just as I was when I finished my career at St Mirren. The doctor told me to quit and warned me I would be a bath-chair job if I didn't.'

And so a great career which had seen Ure winning 11 full caps, was drawing to a close. Many argued he should have won more, but Ure is philosophical and states matter-of-fact that his move to England was the beginning of the end for his international career.

'It was well known that Anglos could be forgotten with home-based players getting preference. I felt this made no sense as my game had improved so much when I went to England — it was superior in every department — and yet I hardly added to my cap collection after going south. And I was never impressed with the way the Scotland team was selected. In 1963 I was part of a makeshift team that went to play Spain in the Bernabu Stadium, home of Real Madrid, and we thrashed them 6-2. I felt I was selected only because others had called off and I wasn't the only one playing that night in that situation.

'And yet we played brilliantly and left the Spaniards

without a whisper of a chance. How many Scotland performances have there been like that over the years? Taking on a crack side and thrashing them in their own back yard. But believe me, most of the men in dark blue that night struggled to be selected again and I think I was only chosen twice more.'

Happily, Dundee's very own 'Big Yogi' would to this day be instantly recognised by all who saw him play. He remains a giant of a man — just like he was in these distant days of glory and greatness.

CHAPTER SIX

Alan Gilzean

IT IS PERHAPS TYPICAL OF ALAN GILZEAN, ONE of the most deadly finishers British football has ever seen, to play down the role which made him a Dens Park hero. His goals in Dundee's march to the league title in 1962 guarantee him immortality status from all who were fortunate enough to witness that golden era when Bob Shankly's Dark Blues climbed to the heights of the domestic game and then came within a whisker of Britain's first European Cup.

Skilful and silky as that famous Dens Park team was, it could be argued that without Gilzean's finishing prowess everlasting fame might well have passed them by. That team was like a machine, essential parts all moving in unison to produce a Rolls Royce, a sleek, prowling, all-powerful piece of work polished by Bob Shankly until it gleamed with pride, until it was ready to move into football's fast lane.

Once Shankly had his model of perfection to his satisfaction, it motored smoothly to the top of the pile, a sleek and awesome football side that left Scotland's lesser models in its slipstream. In terms of converting the class and quality into goals, that vital commodity that separates the winners from the losers, Dundee and Shankly had loaded the dice in their own favour. They had Alan Gilzean although, as many will tell you, there was much more to his repertoire than banging them in and nodding them home. And who could forget the goals, four at Ibrox against a Rangers team feared far and wide? The two at Muirton Park on April 28th, 1962 that finally sent the championship standard to the top of the Dens Park flag pole.

And yet for one member of that glorious Dundee side, that day was tinged with regret and sadness and that was Alan Gilzean. 'It was a big, big day when we went to Muirton. I was the local lad and I had, and still have a lot of friends who are St Johnstone supporters, and the ironic and sad thing for me that day was that poor Saints were relegated. As it turned out a single point would have done us and Saints would have stayed in the First Division. I felt so sorry for them.

'Our pleasure was their grief — there was a touch of that for me, too, probably just because of my local connections.

'Yes, it was a great day on one hand but a sad day on the other. Now that Saints are back in the Premier League with their new stadium and doing so well under Alex Totten, a really nice lad who was at Dens with me, I am ever so pleased for them.

'I was going to travel straight to Perth from Coupar Angus but I thought I'd best go to Dundee because, win, lose or draw, we were going there at night. I recall the Perth road that day was just a mass of traffic and I think Dundee must have had three quarters of the crowd. On the way through to the match we had plenty of time to think of what might lie ahead.

'We all had confidence in our own ability. We knew on paper we were a better team than St Johnstone, the league table proved that — we were at the top and they were close to the bottom. So if we have more ability than they do, all we should be concentrating on doing is looking to win the game, all we really had to do was match them in terms of commitment and effort and if we did that our superior skills would take care of the result and that was exactly what happened.

'I remember that day their left-winger played more like a left back, a lad Thomson, all he was doing was whacking

Smithy and trying to stop him supplying crosses. But Gordon eluded him, got the cross over and I scored my first goal with a header and from that point on, our skill factor did the rest and we ran out good winners.

'My state of mind that day was that if you matched them for effort we would get chances and I was one of the men in the team the rest of the lads relied on to convert these chances into goals.

'And I reckoned over the 90 minutes the way Dundee were playing at that time I would get maybe three or four chances in any given game and I would back myself to score two out of four any time. And that was how it worked.'

And so Alan Gilzean, soon to be a Scotland player, the strolling, hip-swaying hit-man from Coupar Angus had a Scottish League championship medal in his back pocket.

That day vindicated Gilzean's decision to embark on a soccer career with local side Dundee instead of the team he favoured as a boy, Famous-Five inspired Hibs. 'I was with Coupar Angus juveniles, and signed for Dundee on provisional forms. I had the chance to sign for about four clubs, Hibs and Cowdenbeath were also after me, but my father was very keen on Dundee and although I was not a Dundee supporter he reckoned I would not have problems like having to worry about digs.'

Between the years 1957 and 59, this Dundee team was being re-constructed — the golden era of George Anderson was at a close and the vital cogs that were to supply Shankly with his silverware outfit were falling into place. But Gilzean's early days were interrupted by National Service and he played most of his football for his Army unit side at Aldershot, as well as guesting for the Aldershot reserve side.

'During my last six months or so in the Army, Dundee used to bring me up from Aldershot on the Thursday night, I would train on the Friday, play on the Saturday and return on the train on Sunday. It was half-time football and half-time Army but it was a very enjoyable time for me. When I started

Shake on it . . . Cologne defender Benthaus is applauded off Dens Park after the Germans had been thrashed 8-1.

playing regularly for Dundee reserves, I began knocking in a few goals. Unfortunately, in my debut for the first team we were thrashed by a very good Motherwell team, Bert McCann, Pat Quinn and all these guys. It showed me the gulf between reserve and first team football.

'Later in my career I would discover there was the same gulf between first team football and international football. More stamina, more skill, that was always what you needed when stepping up a grade. I had been signed by Willie Thornton and when I played that first game against Motherwell he was still in charge. We lost 4-1 and I never got a kick but Motherwell were one helluva good team at that time, one of the best in Scotland.'

After the arrival of Shankly, Gilzean did not have long to wait for his chance to claim top team football. He was brought on against Liverpool when they arrived to hansel the floodlights at Dens Park, said by the fans to be financed by the sale of Jimmy Gabriel to Everton. That March night in 1960 Dundee beat Liverpool 1-0, Hugh Robertson scoring directly from a corner much to the disgust of Bert Slater in the Liverpool goal.

'I didn't play particularly well and from what I can recall it was a very, very hard game. Liverpool were a tough side, they were battling for promotion from the English Second Division and it was the beginning of the team that Bill Shankly was to build into one of the best, but we managed to win and obviously I had not played too badly or I would not have stayed in. That was my chance, it was at a time Dundee were going through a transitional period. There was still some of the players left from the Billy Steel era, people like Doug Cowie, Albert Henderson, Dave Curtlet — they were gradually phasing them out and whole new breed of players were coming in.

'I always considered it a privilege and pleasure in my first season to play alongside Doug Cowie. To me he was one of the greatest players to have played for the club. He was fantastic.

'I was one of a number of young players coming through — Hammy, George McGeachie, Alan Cousin, Hugh Robertson, Ian Ure — and by that time we had Bobby Seith from Burnley, Bobby Wishart from Aberdeen, and one of my heroes, Gordon Smith, from Hearts.

'Shankly had it off to a fine art, he had the nucleus of a good side and brought in the experienced men, and although Cowie was close to a finish at that stage, Seith, Wishart and Smith gave us the experience we needed to make us into a title-winning combination.

'When Rangers whittled away our comfortable lead and moved in front, Seith, Wishart and Smith calmed things down — their experience meant so much to us during the title run-in.

Champions . . . Surrounded by a sea of fans is Alan Gilzean who has just scored two goals to give Dundee the League title.

Because these lads had all been in that position before, they knew what was required — we had a good blend at Dens, we had bags of skill, we could play football and, if necessary, we could mix it as well.

'We had Ian Ure, Bobby Cox and Bobby Seith who could all look after themselves and we could compete either way. We could do it with brawn, or we could do it with skill and happily it was mostly always with skill. Yes, they were exciting days, for us, for the club, for the fans and exciting for the whole city because it was the first time Dundee had ever risen to such heights. It was a new experience for everyone and the Dundee public responded.'

Who knows, perhaps Gilzean plus other local lads Bobby Cox that inspirational skipper and the silky Bobby Seith from Monifieth, took a special pride in what was happening around the club. Gilzean recalls being taken to Dens as a lad by his father. 'I saw Billy Steel play and he was fantastic. My dad used to take me to Dens — he divided his loyalties between Dundee and St Johnstone supporting both, but obviously Dundee in the Steel era, there was a charisma about the whole club then. George Anderson was a charismatic figure the bowler hat, the bow-tie, the cigar and the walking cane and then with Billy Steel in the team, he was the icing on the cake, especially when they won the two League Cups with Alfie Boyd.

'When I went there at first I can remember Johnny Lynch being in goal, followed by Bill Brown and of course later I played with him at Spurs, Tommy Gallacher, I can remember Danny Malloy before he went to Cardiff City, Ken Zeising, Jimmy Toner. Although I saw Dundee quite a lot, if anything, I was probably attracted more to Hibs, their forward line the Famous Five of Gordon Smith, Bobby Johnstone, Lawrie Reilly, Eddie Turnbull and Willie Ormond. I was drawn to them for what real reason I have no idea. Nobody can say as a kid why you favour a certain team but that was it and I was a kind of Hibs supporter and when I got the chance to go senior it was really between Dundee or Hibs.'

Like all the others, Gilzean worshipped the part played by Bob Shankly and his side-kick Sammy Kean. 'Shankly had been a long time in football. He was with Falkirk and Third Lanark and he came to us from Cathkin where they had a very good side and, who knows, he might have been on the threshold of really good times there because he had players like Dave Hilley, Alex Harley, Matt Gray and Joe McInnes. But he must have looked at Dundee and decided they had more potential than Thirds and obviously, Dundee were the top team in the city at the time and looking at Glasgow you will always have Rangers and Celtic to contend with.

'He was a very fair man, he wanted 100% and if you gave him that he was happy, he criticised — you always have to criticise players but the good thing about Bob was that it was always constructive and I always thought if it was constructive it would do some good and he got that just right. He had a

Number one . . . St Johnstone keeper Taylor is helpless as Gilzean breaks the deadlock at Muirton

good back-up team with Sammy Kean as trainer. Sammy got on very well with the players whereas Shankly had to be that bit more aloof. You need the in-between guy and Sammy was that, him and Lawrie Smith the physio. They both got on really well with the players.

'Sammy was a great character, the joker in the pack. There was never any tension before a match because Sammy would unwind you. He would tell you about the days when he was a defender at Hibs and we would say, but Sammy, Hibs never had a defence, they only had a forward line, and that was why they never really won much. Sammy was a great character and that is what football clubs are all about. It is just not the players on the park, you have to have the right backroom staff.'

The Shankly scenario was falling into place — he had a bunch of young lads prepared to knock the door down to get in about the game's big prizes. Allied to their skill, enthusiasm, and running power was added the old heads and Shankly's brew was on the boil. 'As well as being a good side we were all great pals as well especially the younger ones. We all came in together from the reserves and we all wanted to succeed and, being young, we were prepared to work as hard as necessary to succeed.

'Shankly was a hard man alright, and funnily enough, my next manager in football Bill Nicholson at Spurs, was a hard man too. You have to be hard in football, often you hear of managers who aren't liked and I think that's the way it should be. I believe if a manager is popular there maybe something wrong. Both Bob and Bill Shankly wanted to win things and sometimes you have to be ruthless to achieve that. If you can do it with flair and lovely football that's a bonus. Bob Shankly did it that way and I reckon so too did Billy Nick although funnily enough neither Nicholson nor Shankly were skilled players themselves. They were grafters, hardnuts and that just shows you have to have the blend — you must have skill but you need lads who are prepared to work and run all day and fortunately at Dundee we had just that.'

Gilzean reflects on his team-mates of that time with pride and enthusiasm, none more so than Gordon Smith, one of Scottish football's legends, whose graceful touchline prowl added much to these heady days at Dens. Smith was a nightmare for backs. Such was his artistry on the ball they were reluctant to commit themselves to a tackle, and that gave Gordon the time and the space to swing over a cross with his right or turn inside and float in a hanging ball with his left.

There was every chance — no chance is the wrong word, it was part of the game plan — that Gilzean would be lurking to convert these crosses into priceless goals. A feature of that outfit was the right-wing triangle — a joy to behold.

Alex Hamilton and Bobby Seith, a real gentleman of the game, he never wasted a ball and he had the weighted pass off to fine art proportions.

Andy Penman was another lovely player to watch as the triangle worked its way into danger areas. Often Andy would do Smith's running for him and when a full back saw the Smith-Penman duo approaching he would very often wish he'd gone shopping with his missus. In full flight, Penman had the grace of a Puma and when given the job of converting a penalty kick he added the stealth of an alley-cat.

But this was no one-sided operation, far from it. Down the left was wee Hugh Robertson, Shug to one and all, and Bobby Wishart, brought from Aberdeen in the twilight of his career. Wishart kicked a mean dead ball and his shooting was forever a threat when the enemy goal came into view. Wee Shug, his legs going like pistons, would dodge and dance through defences to make the Dark Blue assault force a double-edged sword.

'Gordon Smith was just fantastic and the contribution he made was tremendous. He was an internationalist, a world class player and I believe he never got the caps he should have had when he played with the Hibs and it is amazing when he moved to Hearts and Dundee he got championship medals with each of them too. He was a great influence, and obviously the other four in the forward line were all youngsters and so his influence was very welcome.

'Hugh Robertson was a little terrier, he had a lot of skill on the ball but he did not have power for taking people on at pace but was very very tricky, he could turn on a sixpence. These days were just the beginning of the over-lapping full back but few of Hugh's opponents got that chance, because he would always be at their heels chasing and snapping. That again was balance and that was again Shankly at his best. On one side he had a little terrier, turning quick, darting here and there and on the other Smith, the stylist, with crosses and feints.

'The work Alan Cousin did was fantastic. We were a very good partnership, I was very lucky, I did the striking role at that time and he was doing all the grafting, laying balls on and when I moved to Spurs my role was reversed — I was doing the

laying on and a lad called Jimmy Greaves was doing the
scoring, you have to get the right blend, the right striking
partnership and in my career I was very lucky having Alan
Cousin at Dens Park and Jimmy Greaves at White Hart Lane.

'Alan Cousin was very much under-rated. He had two
options of course, he was at St Andrews University going for
his first class honours MA and obviously his academic career
was more important to him than football. We only saw him as
a full-timer during the school holidays but he was a great player
and a fine fellow.

'I am sure if he had dedicated himself to football he would
have been every bit as good as I was and maybe even better
because he had fantastic pace. He was only part-time as I said
but stamina-wise he was fantastic and that more than anything
else looked after the guys behind him, guys like Seith and
Wishart.'

If Gilzean's status as a Dens Park hero was ever in doubt,
these vanished on the November day when Dundee demolished
Rangers 5-1 at Ibrox. 'It was obviously going to be a hard test
for us because Rangers seemed to be our main rivals for the
title, but we had a confidence about us and we felt we were as
good if not better than any side in the league, we had a run of
really good victories behind us and that day at Ibrox we just
took Rangers apart. Honestly, it could have been seven or
eight. I scored four that day and it is easy to say it was down to
me but forwards always get the glory and defensively we played
very, very well too.'

That result convinced the supporters and perhaps the
players that a Championship triumph was Dundee's for the
asking but it was a week later before Shankly himself was
convinced that something big was about to happen. That day
unfancied Raith Rovers came to Dens and stormed into a 4-2
lead with only 15 minutes remaining. Gillie did has bit with the
first two goals but the heroes came from elsewhere when the
chips were down and a Kirkcaldy victory looked a certainty.
Bobby Wishart's power drive reduced the deficit to 4-3, his

Pick it out . . . Gilzean outflanks Killie's Frank Beattie to score one of his goals in the Scottish Cup semi at Ibrox.

wing-half partner Bobby Seith made it 4-4 with only four minutes remaining and then with Raith keeper Willie Cunningham, an ex-Dundee player, wishing he was home by the fireside, Gordon Smith hit the winner with just 120 seconds left on the clock. It was a vital result, a vital win, a watershed of Dundee's title ambitions.

Gilzean recalls yet another vital match as Dundee played an Easter Monday derby against Dundee United at Tannadice.

'I remember that game well, we beat United 2-1 and I scored both. The first was definitely thanks to United keeper Rolando Ugolini, I hit a speculative shot from 25 yards out and it took a bounce just before it got to Rolando and he dived over the top of it! The second was from about 20 yards and it screamed right into the top corner — that was a very difficult game for us.'

The role played by Pat Liney in that championship season should never be under-estimated, he was rock solid from start to spectacular finish and ever-present which in itself tells a story. Gilzean reflected with sadness at the way Liney slipped from the top team into obscurity, replaced in that close season after the magic of Muirton by little Bert Slater, who was to play such a key role in the European Cup campaign.

'There is no doubt Pat was very unlucky to be discarded after winning the championship medal. I put his plight in the same category as a guy at Spurs, a centre forward called Les Allen who scored over 20 goals when Tottenham won the double. And the next season he was in the reserves because the club brought Jimmy Greaves back from Italy. I feel very sad for Les Allen just as I do for Pat Liney. Through no fault of his own a player becomes second choice but again that gets back to management, that's what being a manager is all about making tough decisions, you have to be ruthless and who is to say that Shankly was right or wrong when he replaced Pat Liney. If you saw Bert Slater performing in Europe and in that Cup Final against Rangers, you would have to say that Shankly's decision was right. But who is to say that Pat would not have performed just as well. Who knows?'

In Continental terms Dundee had to grow up fast and Gilzean subscribes to the theory that the learning process began during that summer of 1962 when they took part in the New York tournament. And he, too, has horrible memories of the return against Cologne in West Germany, in the European Cup first round.

It's there . . . Gilzean scores his second at Muirton leaving the Saints defence helpless.

'All the aggro was a throw-back to the first leg at Dens when their goalie was carried off, a guy called Fritz Ewert, but it was a pure accident. I think he hit Alan Cousin's knee and was concussed and had double vision. The Germans tried to make a lot out of that, but big Alan wouldn't kick anybody, he was a real gentleman. But the German press made it look that we had deliberately gone to hurt their goalkeeper.

'After all, Cologne had been favourites to win the cup and they had some explaining to do to their supporters. They had just lost 8-1 to a team from Scotland that nobody had heard of and all they could come up with was that Dundee had deliberately put the goalkeeper out of the game. So the anger was there right from the start in Germany and everyone who was there will remember it as a horrible experience.

'In the next round we were drawn against Sporting Lisbon and although we lost 1-0 in Portugal they were a small side and

I knew we would take care of them at Dens and we did quite comfortably. Then it was Anderlecht and we played really well in the Heysel Stadium. Yes, I played well for the club that night even though I had to go to the hospital after the game to have six stitches put in a cut above my ankle. I scored two and we played really well as a team, they were throwing a lot at us and we were scoring on the counter.

'Again that night the forwards took a lot of the credit but defensively we were outstanding. But then we were found out against AC Milan. We were doing well in the first half in the San Siro but, after half time, we lost bad goals. They had a guy called Barison at outside left and they were drawing big Ian out of position and hitting this lad with high balls. He was up against Hammy and no way could Hammy compete with this lad in the air. But they were a very good side, they had Altafini and Gianna Rivera, Maldini the centre half and Trapattoni.

'They were a class side, for some reason they seemed to single me out for some rough treatment. I had a little guy called Benitez marking me and all he did was follow me all over the park, gobbing on me, kicking me but you will always get that and you have to come to expect these things.

'Unfortunately, when we got them back at Dens I eventually lost my head, and was sent off. Italians are always the same — just ask Denis Law or Greavesie — anyone who has played in Italy and they will tell you that is how the game if played. They try and get to you but you have to be above that and unfortunately that night at Dens I wasn't. I saw red mist, the guy was whacking me all over the place then someone was whacking Gordon Smith and I could take no more. The referee saw it all and said "my decision is out." I will never forget his words and I had to go. The referee should have nailed all the bother early on and it would have been a good game. Okay, we would not have won the tie because a 5-1 deficit from the first leg was too great — you could never give that kind of start to the Italians, perhaps the Portuguese, but not the Italians, they are masters of defence, man-for-man marking and they went on to win the cup.'

Off night . . . Mayhem against Milan in the incident that led to Gilzean's dismissal.

Gilzean's next season was to be his last full term with the club — by that time the international scene had beckoned and Gillie was playing for Scotland on a bigger stage with players who enjoyed bigger pay packets. The time was drawing nigh for the tall local hero   he would soon ply his trade on a bigger stage. But before then there was more domestic glory to bid for and that season climaxed with what became known as Slater's final.

'The year we won the League, I think I scored about 23 goals but the season after, I was on target more than 50 times, there were many good Cup games that season although I scored six in the League against Queen of the South at Dens — mind you they had goalkeeper George Farm carried off that day.

'The Cup run saw Dundee take nine off Brechin at Glebe Park and six off neighbours Forfar at Dens. Then in the quarter-finals there was a dramatic tie against Motherwell, Joe McBride scored an equaliser with the ref's watch in overtime and so it was on to Fir Park for a Wednesday replay. A 25,000 crowd saw Dundee winning a thrilling encounter by 4-2. The next hurdle on the way to Hampden was against Kilmarnock at Ibrox, a happy hunting ground for Alan Gilzean and so it proved as the Dark Blues triumphed 4-0.

There was a huge 120,982 crowd at Hampden for the final and only the Dundee element left disappointed, but they had seen a dramatic match. Little Slater, Bob Shankly's ace card in the European Cup campaign, had a marvelous match, defying Rangers single-handed and breaking their hearts until the dying moments.

'It was 1-1 for a long time, Kenny Cameron having scored for Dundee and I had a good chance to put us ahead but Ronnie McKinnon blocked my effort and unfortunately I injured my ankle. Little Bert played brilliantly that day and he kept us in the match but there was nothing he could do as Rangers scored two late goals to make it 3-1.'

By that time, Gilzean had made up his mind to go.

'You play international football and you realise what other people are earning and obviously the first one of that great Dundee side who thought he could do better was big Ian. He obviously said to himself "I have had two or three great years at Dundee and now I must cash in." The club can only pay players what they are bringing through the turnstiles. Nowadays there are sponsorship deals and commercial earnings, but not then, and that meant unfortunately Bob Shankly was just coming to the stage when he couldn't offer us any more.

'It starts when you get into the international team. I used to room with John White when he was with Tottenham and he would tell me what he was earning and I would tell him what I was getting and believe me there was a big, big difference. Eventually, you would come to the conclusion that you would have to move and unfortunately that was the break up of a great Dundee team. At that time there were no long-term contracts, you signed on every year and I came to the end of my contract and I had talks with Shanks to see if he could come up with terms that would suit me. But in my heart of hearts I knew I had to go because I thought at the time the team was beginning to break up and if you recall the history of Dundee, they don't win things on a regular basis every two or three years. Winning cups and trophies, there were always long spells in between from the Scottish Cup win back in 1910, to the Billy Steel era in the early 1950s, to the championship side of 1962 and you say to yourself, God Almighty it might be a long, long time before it happens again.

'Obviously, I was an internationalist by then and I thought that might even affect my position for Scotland, so I had to decide it was time to go. But Dundee did not want to sell me so the only course open for me was to go on the dole. And so it went on until Shankly eventually phoned to say they had a buyer. He wanted to sell me to Sunderland for £62,000 the same money that took Ian Ure to Arsenal but I wouldn't go. I had always said that in England there were the big five, the two Liverpool teams, Manchester United, Spurs and Arsenal, they were the big clubs and I wanted one of them.'

At times like this, with Alan Gilzean in dispute with the club, you could imagine fans sitting at school desks and praying that no-one would come in for Gillie. He would then get fed up not playing, return to Dens, and pick up a long and glorious career. But youngsters with these thoughts were on a loser, for it just doesn't work out like that, as outside forces — the Mr Fix-its of the game — make it their business to arrange things.

'There was this reporter called Jim Roger, they call him scoop, he is a real good lad and he was very friendly with Bill Nick and he always told me Spurs were keen — he fixed it for me. I refused to sign for Sunderland — I would rather go and get a job outside football than do that but unfortunately I was never tested on that promise. I played in the John White testimonial for Scotland at White Hart Lane and we murdered them and within two weeks I was signed for Spurs. The money was better and it was a good challenge, it is okay saying you could have stayed and made Dundee a great side again but you don't know how it would have worked and Tottenham were in a transitional period too. It was just like when I joined at Dens. Spurs would go on to great things and win trophies. We won the F.A. Cup in 1967 when we beat Chelsea in the final and in the early 1970s we won the League Cup two years on the trot, we won the UEFA Cup one year and were beaten finalists the next.

'You are only what the people want you to be and they could make you or break you. The Tottenham crowd are fickle and they will either take to you or they don't, and happily they took to me. They loved me and I will always be grateful for that. Curiously, they hated Terry Venables, they used to boo him and if took a corner and put it into the side netting, they would cheer sarcastically.

'When I went there I was fortunate to strike up a very good partnership with Jimmy Greaves in a very good side and happily I became one of the Spurs idols, I can't put my finger on it and say why but naturally I am very pleased it happened that way.

'Jimmy was fantastic to play with, he is the best finisher I have ever seen. He had half a second more than anyone else. As a finisher, dribbling at pace and getting the ball past the keeper, he was the tops.

'I can always remember going down with Dundee to see Scotland playing at Wembley when we won 2-1, Ian Ure was playing and that was the day Eric Caldow broke his leg, Ian Ure was fast but once in a race for the ball with Greavesie you could see big Ian's neck straining. But Jimmy was by him and that was just an indication how fast the little man was and more important he could do it with the ball at his feet. He was a great player and he is an unbelievable character. He always had this ability when he was through on goal, he could commit the goalkeeper and make him do exactly what he wanted to make it easy for him, it was like the ball was tied to his shoelace. We had a gymnasium with little ice hockey goals and some of the best skill I have ever seen from Greavesie was when he would go through five or six players in the space of four yards with the ball at his feet.'

Alan Gilzean has many happy memories from his days as a Scotland player when he won caps, and one of his best was when he scored the winner against England at Hampden in 1964. 'It was a very, very wet day and a very close game, I had a couple of chances, I hit one really well but Ron Springett made a very good save. My opponent was Maurice Norman later a team-mate at Spurs, this corner came over from the left, I got there first headed it down and it was in the back of the net, that was a great feeling. My biggest regret at that level was not getting to the World Cup Finals. I always felt we had the ability, but perhaps lacked the teamwork or pattern. Germany knocked us out to go to Mexico in 1970, we played well in Hamburg that night but Tommy Gemmell unfortunately gave away a silly penalty. Mind you after I came out of the international scene, Scotland have hardly missed the World Cup Finals so who knows maybe it was down to me — maybe I was the bad link!'

Oh, how Scotland could have used a Gilzean in full-flight in 1974 when we were ubeaten in three first phase matches but failed to go through because of our inability to convert outfield superiority into goals. Something tells me that Gilzean might have been able to do something about that, but we will never know.

All who saw Alan Gilzean will be grateful for his grace, his clinical finishing, his magnificent heading ability, but the player, too, is grateful for the part football has played in his life.

'Any young lad wishing to be a footballer could not have wished for any better than what I got. I was part of the Dundee team that made history and later I was part of a very successful Tottenham team. In between, I played for Scotland. I was always fortunate, I have never played with teams that have not been successful so they were all great times. You can see some guys who never had that. I was at Wembley three times with Spurs and once with Scotland, I had a Cup Final day at Hampden, kids at school dream about that and for some it comes true and for others unfortunately it goes wrong. Yes, I always wanted a career like that but it is in the lap of the Gods.

'The Dundee thing was a part of my life I am very proud of. I am probably now a dual supporter, Dundee and Tottenham but obviously I am am closer to Tottenham and I was longer there, 10 years compared to five years at Dens Park so obviously the calling for Tottenham is greater. And it is more recent as well and with my son Ian being on the staff there I will always be close to them but Dundee will always have a fond place in my heart.'

CHAPTER SEVEN

Charlie Cooke

ON PAPER, CHARLIE COOKE'S CREDENTIALS TO be remembered as one of the great Dundee players hardly stand up to close examination. He joined the club with just a few days left of 1964 and left again as 1966 was still in its infancy. If every player followed that behaviour pattern, the revolving doors at the entrance to the land's soccer stadiums would need oiled on a daily basis.

Stretching the point, it was just over a year and a bit, and during that time no heather was set on fire, no records were broken and no silverware found its way to the Dens Park trophy room. Indeed, an examination of the record books during his stay between December '64 and April '66 would be remarkable only for some exceptional results, but certainly not for any hint of title-winning form. And if you looked really closely, you might discover some lingering evidence that Dundee were in fact entered for the two Scottish Cup campaigns graced by Cooke in the Dark Blue jersey.

At the first time of asking Bob Shankly's men, proud Hampden participants of a thrilling Final encounter just a matter of months before, tumbled ungraciously to St Johnstone at Muirton at the first hurdle involving the so-called big-guns. And 12 months later the Dark Blues went only one stage further, falling 2-0 to Celtic at Dens after promising something a bit more exciting than that thanks to the 9-1 tanking of East Fife in Dundee.

So how come this guy who seemed to drift along the very edge of Dundee Football Club's proud tradition is up there with the best? That's easy, just ask anyone who saw Charlie play and they'll tell you how it was. For this Cooke was Cordon Bleu material — a class act who had the Dens Park fans eating from the palm of his hand. There can't be many players who flit through a club as he did and lay claim to a status normally reserved for Cup-winning heroes or flag-grabbing champions.

On paper, the argument for Cooke's inclusion in our Hall of Fame is flimsy. On the park, there is no argument at all, for he was, without fear of contradiction, one of the top men. His arrival made Christmas of 1964 a much happier one for all Dundee fans, who just days earlier had seen their No. 1 hero Alan Gilzean hit the transfer trek Down South. Cooke's was the kind of signing that would placate the restless Dark Blue support which was witnessing the break-up of an all-conquering team of giants.

True, the remnants of that 1961-62 outfit were still on the scene — men like Alex Hamilton, Bobby Cox, Bobby Seith, Alan Cousin, and Andy Penman. But gone were Gordon Smith and Bobby Wishart into well-earned retirement, Ian Ure, lost to the lure of the Big Smoke and now the much-loved Gillie to the other half of North London's Old Firm.

The signing of Charlie Cooke for £40,000 from Aberdeen was a masterstroke by the Dens hierarchy, but, to this day, the player himself gets his dander up at any talk of him being 'Gilzean's replacement'. 'I don't mean to sound disrespectful to Alan Gilzean but I never had the slightest inferiority complex about him or anyone else and I don't give a s − − − how many goals he scored. People said I was there to replace Alan but I never saw it that way. I recall thinking "If I'm here to replace Alan Gilzean, you've got a bargain boys." That was the kind of feeling I had, deep down a kind of confidence that I don't think I would ever articulate but that was my feeling — maybe it was cockiness that I didn't realise I had.'

Wizardry . . . Cooke takes England's Keith Newton for a walk.

Of course, comparing the players, Cooke and Gilzean were both top-drawer performers but their styles were poles apart. And the Dundee Board of Directors, anxious to please the support, played an ace card when they persuaded Aberdeen to part with their golden boy, and it didn't take long for Cooke to get the smile back on the faces of the Dundee support as Charlie won them over in an instant with his magical concoction of ball skills and wizardry.

Cooke was an individualist on the park and he remains an individualist to this day as he expounds his vision of the football dream in his capacity as US-Canada Director of Coerver Coaching. One of the game's thinkers, he is still aiming for the impossible dream . . . to make soccer a beautiful game once more, to restore the emphasis to skill and artistry.

He had that in abundance from an early age and it would surely have been rewarded in the shape of international honours but for the perversity, as he saw it, of a school gym teacher, who had better remain anonymous.

'As a youngster maybe I was reclusive — I don't know — but I never had the inclination that I needed a lot of company. If I wanted to do something I just went and did it, and at that time I think soccer became something of an obsession with me. I played for my school team at Primary level and when I went up to Greenock High School I was in the team right through to the third year. Then I got the chance to play for an under-age team called Port Glasgow Rovers and that was a big deal — I thought I was a star.'

Like so many youths of these days, Cooke was happy to play for his school side on Saturday mornings then rush off to do it again in the afternoons. But this was the point where the gym teacher intervened. 'There was no conflict, but for some reason he said that I had to choose — it was either playing for the school team or Port Rovers — I couldn't do both. Now playing for the Rovers seemed like pro soccer to me and there was no hard choice to be made — in my eyes they were big time. But I learned later that this teacher put the ultimatum to me in the knowledge that I was to go for trials to play for Scotland schoolboys. That wasn't in my wildest dreams — I just wanted to play, good, bad or indifferent, but he made me choose without telling me about the trial.

'I remember thinking "what kind of sick guy is this" but at the time it didn't upset me that much because I was still so proud to be playing for Port Rovers. Subsequently, when we were having trials for the school athletics team and in the sprint heats, me and my buddies would all go out for 75 yards and then with the tape in sight we'd all slow up and allow lesser runners to beat us. That meant the gym teacher had to select them instead of us and we thought that was smart — although looking back it was really a stupid way to behave. I don't think I was evil as a kid but he did something to me that really turned me against him — but I think it was a pretty poor bit of adult behaviour on his part.'

That meant that the young Cooke's participation in school sporting events was brought to a premature close but his

Fooled again . . . This time it's England ace Martin Peters who faces the Cooke magic.

football career took the next step forward because of what he was doing on the field with Port Glasgow Rovers. 'I was only there a short while and then I was playing at about 15½ for Port Glasgow Juniors, alongside real men, old pros who would kick the s − − − out of you. They would all be fighting and kicking opponents but me, I just wanted to play football — it was really bizarre, me just a slip of a boy in a team with an average of about 25. They even let me take all the penalties.'

Before attracting the attention of the seniors, Cooke signed for Renfrew Juniors who had a good reputation for signing young hopefuls and passing them on to greater things. 'They were a kind of nursery team because they always wanted to make their money, that was how they survived. At the time I was getting paid about 17s 6d and I would go home and give my mum five bob which would leave me with twelve bob to go and get drunk with my buddies, who all worked in the shipyard.'

Then an amazing thing happened to Cooke that had him shaking his head in disbelief as he told the story all these years and memories later. 'Aberdeen had shown an interest and their scout Bobby Calder came to a match and I agreed that I would go up to Pittodrie to let them have a look at me. A week later Calder came back to a Renfrew game to confirm the arrangements and that was fine. But not long before the match started the Renfrew manager called me aside and introduced me to this Rangers scout, who was well-known for signing good players from the junior ranks.

'We shook hands and he asked me if I would be interested in going up to Ibrox to meet Mr Struth sometime that week. Can you believe the words that came out of my mouth right there and then — "I am very sorry sir, but I have just agreed with Mr Calder to go up to Aberdeen." Believe me 20 years later you wouldn't have heard these words. "Would I like to go and see Mr Struth? — don't go away, give me your telephone number, let's get this sorted out here and now" — that would have been my response. But how was that for innocence abroad — naive in the extreme.

'When I look back at that I think I must have been crazy. It wasn't as if I had my father at my side giving me advice and I remember it was all very honourable, the Renfrew manager didn't try to influence me at all and the Rangers scout politely accepted what I had said and didn't try and twist my arm in any way. So that was it — forget Rangers, and Aberdeen here I come but it didn't make me unhappy. It's terrible but I didn't give a s– – – that Rangers were interested, I was just so excited about going to a senior club.'

Cooke's first game in a Dons jersey was against Clyde reserves and it was an eye-opening experience if only for reasons that were maybe disappointing. 'George Herd was playing for Clyde and he was magnificent, he was special, but him apart, I remember thinking that none of the others were much good. There was me running my ass off and all these old pros . . . I don't mean to be snide but . . .' The criticism tails off as it would be regarded as disrespectful but the experience gave Cooke the confidence to go boldly into his new career. Not that boldness or confidence were in short supply.

'After I'd joined the full-time staff I played in Aberdeen's public trial which was nothing really except for all the young hopefuls. I think I was a bit of a sensation because I was beating people all over the place and it was as if everyone was saying ''Who the hell is this kid?'' That was the kind of impact I made but that was my game — I was a dribbler and I'd think nothing of beating five or six men. Looking back I must have been pretty good at it although beating people takes enormous energy and I used to just about kill myself. But I loved doing it and I couldn't get enough of it — I was just the same way in practice.'

The Transatlantic use of the word practice when most would use training gives a clue about Cooke's views on soccer which shaped his destiny when his playing days were over. But more of that later.

Cooke's arrival on the Pittodrie scene was quite exceptional. And within a few weeks of his joining the full-timers he was the talk of the pubs from Union Street to King Street. He brought a freshness to the scene and a devil-may-care approach. But he was a Cavalier flanked by Round Heads and the mediocrity of his Aberdeen team-mates only served to underline just how good this slim young man was going to be. Remember, this was an age when Pittodrie crowds were poor and, if truth be told, the team wasn't that special either . . . except for two or three with Charlie Cooke to the fore.

'I got into the Scotland Under-23 team and I played for the Scottish League against the Italian League in Rome and that was something of an achievement, as most of the young players breaking through at that level were with either Rangers or Celtic. I recall playing the Italian League against guys like John Charles and Helmut Haller in the Olympic Stadium. I went back to our hotel after the game and I was totally drained. I was physically sick with fatigue having run my legs off. I was just over-whelmed with anxiety and although we lost 4-2 I scored with a header.'

This is another clue into the Cooke make-up — the cockiness was not quite so up front when he had a point to prove. Cooke at that time was staying in digs, training, or should I say practising hard, and doing his best to make an impact on the professional game. He was happy enough at Aberdeen and off the park he was having the time of his life. But fame beckoned and fame meant a move and, although it might sound strange these days, progress was a move down the road to Dens Park.

'There was maybe a lack of ambition about Pittodrie but that was no fault of the people there. After all, we are talking about Aberdeen, they wanted the club to make a few bucks and not lose a few bucks. It was like Renfrew and, in retrospect, it was the best place to go as a kid because they were looking to move good players on.

'I forget my real reason for wanting to leave Pittodrie but it boils down to ambition and, although I tried to force their hand, I wasn't ambitious in the way I later saw other players, conniving and pulling off shrewd tricks to get what they wanted out of the game. I was never like that, I was naive to the enth degree.

'There wasn't much difference between Aberdeen and Dundee. I remember Andy Penman was a real moody boy and

By the right . . . Charlie Cooke in action for Chelsea.

he always had this thing with the management about wanting a transfer and wanting to go and play for Rangers. I think he asked for a move just as I arrived at Dens — it had all been brewing for some time — and I remember thinking when I met him and got to know what he could do, "You are no problem, I don't give a s – – – if you leave." I had been a great admirer of Penman, Alan Cousin and Alan Gilzean as a trio when I had played against them because Dundee had stuffed us a couple of times and remember thinking they were pretty special. Maybe I was a bit in awe of Andy because I thought he was as gifted a player as I had seen — he was a great finisher, a lovely striker of the ball, a good, comfortable dribbler and pretty quick — a smart player I thought. When I arrived I came with a bit of a reputation but Andy and Alex Hamilton, they were the cocks of the walk at Dens. But as soon as we got out on the practice ground I thought I could forget these two right away.'

Cooke's choice of language might sound strange but, against the background of dressing room patter and an individual's need to assert his personality on his team-mates, you might begin to get an understanding.

'It maybe took a wee bit longer to sort out Andy but I knew they were never going to be a threat to me. They couldn't stop me — not that they had any reason or motive to do so. They didn't have clay feet or bad habits, it was just that they weren't what I thought they were and remember, these guys were big names. I found out they weren't all they were cracked up to be and I became more and more convinced that this was going to be easier than maybe I thought it would be.'

'But I settled in very quickly, and happily, I established a rapport with the support similar to that which I enjoyed at Pittodrie. One of the things that made me feel at home was that I bought a house in Broughty Ferry and Bobby Cox had his bar down there. And I got hooked up with Coxer and a couple of his friends and we used to do a lot of fishing, and go shooting with dogs and all that. I remember having to build a big, brick wall at the back of my house, and I was as fit as a fiddle — as fit as I ever was in my life.

Cooke in the Dark Blue at an under-populated Firhill.

'I can remember playing against Celtic at Dens Park and I think it was a draw. But I remember that night it was almost as if I was on drugs — and I have never touched drugs in my life — but I remember running and dribbling non stop and yapping to the likes of Tommy Gemmell, threatening him and running rings around him and saying to another Celtic player — "You're next pal." It wasn't bravado, it was just a cockiness — I was going about saying "You? you are nothing" and at that time I think I could have done well anywhere and I could recalls lots of other times when I never felt anything like that.

'But maybe that was my time when you get to the absolute peak of your physical power. I felt as if I was unstoppable and, although it sounds terrible now, my state of mind then was "I don't give a s – – – who you are, you can't stop me."

'Dundee was a good time in my life, I felt awfully good about my soccer and I thought some of the best games I played were around that time and I liked the people who were around me — especially Bobby Cox and some of the people I had got to know in Broughty Ferry.

'It just seemed like a nice time although I must admit I did feel it was only temporary. While I was there I was going to enjoy myself and enjoy my soccer but I always felt I was going somewhere else, wherever it may be.' Cooke becomes embarrassed when he recalls the link between his departure from Aberdeen and then Dundee. 'Talk about history repeating itself. Both times, I was given the supporters' Player-of-the-Year award and I was away the next morning. I would pick up these awards and say "Thank you so much, this means so much to me" and it was goodnight and gone. Now, looking back, I think what I did was pretty nasty.'

It was while at Dens Park though that Cooke won full international recognition and after starring in a 4-1 win over Wales at Hampden he was in for the ill-fated World Cup decider against Italy in Naples. Jock Stein's Scots lost 3-0 and Cooke remembers it only as a bad experience.

There were some happier experiences for Cooke in the

Dark Blue of Dundee. Who could forget his debut performance against struggling Airdrie at Dens when he inspired the late Alex Harley to a rare hat-trick and then iced the cake with a goal of his own. The Dens choir sang 'Charlie is my darling' and that meant a new hero was being shaped. The displays from Dens Park's slim-line tonic were from a different planet but results were indifferent, although the whole of Scottish football sat up and took notice when Hearts were murdered 7-1 at Tynecastle with Andy Penman and the deadly Kenny Cameron each getting a treble.

The new season 1965-66 brought a similar pattern and it must be said that Cooke could be anonymous too. He was just that on the day Jim McLean made his debut for the club at outside left when, horror of horrors, Dundee United gave Dundee five without reply one sunny but miserable day. Cooke was an occasional goal scorer and his last counters for the club came in the form of a double against Stirling Albion in a 6-2 victory just a few weeks before his departure.

His scoring prowess — or lack of it as his career developed — prompts more interesting Cooke views. 'I don't really know if this happened to other players in the game but when I first started playing senior football I was scoring quite a few. One season at Aberdeen I scored over 15 goals and was second top marksman. But then people kept telling me I was a schemer and I went down to maybe 10 or 11 a season. Then it was about eight and then, at a time when I was becoming more experienced and a better player, the goals dried up to a level of about four a season. It was as if subconsciously I didn't need to score because of this schemer tag. My thinking might have been — wait a minute, I don't score them, I just lay them on. You don't realise at the time that these things happen but all the schemer talk had a very big part in how I played the game.'

The major aspect of Cooke's repertoire was his amazing dribbling ability — right foot or left, he could make the ball sit up and talk, with opponents invariably left on the seat of their pants. 'I always used to work hard at practice and from day one I have never cut corners. Maybe I did overdo it at times but I felt in super shape and was often looking for people to come and try to get the ball from me. Everybody told me I should part with the ball quicker than I did and maybe they were right. But at the time I just wanted to be better than I was, I just wanted to beat someone another way, beat another two men and that would make me happy and once I had beaten them I would want to put the ball in the net and that would be just great.' Then, with a boyish laugh, Cooke would scoff: 'Of course it hardly ever worked out like that.

'My game took enormous energy and anyone who saw me play could tell when I had overdone the ball work when I would crouch down with both knees bent and my right hand supporting me. That was when I was done in.'

Like all geniuses, Cooke had his ups and downs at the very top level but one Scotland game he recalls with pride was when a very strong England side was held at a 1-1 draw at Hampden in 1968. 'I was at the peak of my fitness and I can remember running past Alan Ball and saying "Get out of my way." It's a terrible attitude to have, isn't it, but that was how I felt that day. I would be thinking — where is the next problem because he is not a problem. We dominated the game much more than we had done in recent years and although we didn't win it was regarded as a moral victory. But after the game Alf Ramsey said that I had hurt Scotland as much as I had hurt England. I think he was inferring that I had overcarried the ball but I wasn't interested. I remember thinking — Alf Ramsey? He's just another f – – – – – gym teacher.'

Cooke's Chelsea career had more highs than lows — he won an English Cup medal in 1970 and then capped that with a European Cup-Winners' triumph against Real Madrid in Athens in season 1970-71. He expresses disgust at his lack of recall of big events. 'The Chelsea v Leeds Cup Final was a big event in my life but, do you know something, I had forgotten the game went to a replay at Old Trafford. I only remembered when someone sent me a video a couple of years back. Some

Cooke proudly wears the Dark Blue of Scotland.

bits of the game I could recall but most of it, I didn't know it had happened. It was like being at the match — but there I was playing in it.

'That's why I would say to people that big events should be signposted. It's only by making a big thing of them that you are able to remember later on. Your memory should strike chords and you should be able to make the most of the highs, and tie robbons and bows on events and make the big ones even bigger.

'But that was never the way I did it. I can't remember playing in the English Cup Final — that's pathetic, I think it's awful. And I struggle to remember people I played with — who's this Sammy Wilson character — I think that's shocking.

'When we won the Cup I remember sitting on the open-deck bus with my buddy Tommy Baldwin saying — "OK we've won the Cup — let's go to the bar." All the others were making the most of the occasion but I was lucky if I put my hands on the Cup once. I think that's a great shame as I didn't get as much out of these moments as I should have.'

Cooke's status as an all-time Stamford Bridge hero is a measure of the huge impact he made but it wasn't like that for every Dens Parker who took the transfer trail south. Iain Phillip joined Crystal Palace at the same time as Cooke in 1972 but his stay was destined to be a short one and, happily, Iain, the quiet, canny local boy called Aggie because he preferred an Agatha Christie read to a game of cards on the team bus, came back to Dens in time to pick up a League Cup Winners' medal.

'Palace was a bit of a shambles and Iain had a bit of a nightmare down there. I didn't do much and Iain had a difficult time too. He seemed a step slower and a thought slower when in fact he wasn't. Sometimes when people are away from home they just don't feel right and I always had that feeling about Iain.

'A lot of my Chelsea career gave me a great time particularly when I still had that competitive instinct — nothing and no-one could put me down and I felt great about myself. But for the last eight or nine years of my career I didn't feel so good about myself — it was second-rate rubbish. What soured me was all the bullshit I read, heard or saw. Some of the Chelsea players were very talented and they deserved all the credit they got. But some of the others, well . . . All the time people were talking about this wonderful team, these wonderful players. I knew it was all phoney, some of the players were cheating like crazy and I think that was the beginning of my feelings about how the game should be played.

'To say I was disillusioned sounds pathetic but maybe I was. It sounds like a huge excuse for a second-rate player and maybe that was what I was by then. Anyway, when I look back I am surprised I survived as long as I did considering the way I felt about all that rubbish.

'I used to cringe when people called me an entertainer. I wanted people to think I was a productive player and a good man to have in the team. Deep down I just think you are living out your soccer fantasies and I felt a good player was many different things. I wanted people to think I was smart, courageous, entertaining, dangerous a lot of different things and the term "entertainer" is just a quick-line description by people who are being lazy.'

'I want the game to be rid of all the hammer throwers and so-called tough guys with no skill. People say it's a man's game but they're not men, they're just big babies. They have no skill and all they can do is kick people up in the air.'

Cooke is not one of these old pros who drifts back to the good old days and bemoans the passing of distant eras. Clearly, he mourns not for the passing of his era as a player and, unlike most, he is now trying to do his bit to bring change.

From his home base in Cincinnati, Cooke's mission is to work on skill through practice, practice and more practice. 'We are not trying to cultivate pansies and if I am trying to do anything it is to develop players who are just as tough as the next guy but players who can blind opponents with skill and technique. If you want to play tough, we'll play tough too, but give us the ball and you are going to be a frightened player.

'Weil Coerver was a Dutch First Division player who, when he became a coach, couldn't understand why he couldn't develop attacking players by making them better and more dangerous. He looked at some of the game's greatest attacking players, analysed what they did and broke it down. And as sure as a gun is a pistol, the performance and capability of individual players improved beyond recognition by constant practice. I thought this guy hit the nail on the head — he struck a chord with me.'

So Charlie Cooke, looking as fit as ever he was, is plunged headlong into a programme designed to produce better and more skilful players and by an extension of that aim, better, more entertaining and more exciting games.

'When you go to a game you go hoping you're going to see something special, something exciting, someone who can take your breath away. You want to see skills that make you say "Boy, that guy is good — surely this is what the game is all about." That is Charlie Cooke talking . . . but it could just as easily have been someone talking about Charlie Cooke. Thanks for the memories, Charlie, and that's no bullshit.

CHAPTER EIGHT

Jocky Scott

WHEN THE STORY OF DUNDEE FOOTBALL CLUB comes to be written, there will be many with claims for a locker in the Dark Blue Hall of Fame. Majestic, ball-players, inspirational match-winners, classy entertainers, coaches and managers with brilliant tactical brains.

Not many will fit neatly into all of the aforementioned categories — but Jocky Scott does just that.

In his 22 years with the Dens Park club, Jocky has been all of these things in a career that has spanned the peaks and the troughs from the heady, hopeful days of 1964 all the way through, with only the briefest interruption, to his departure from the manager's hot-seat in gloomy circumstances in 1988.

It's perhaps difficult to appreciate that Jocky was to the fore for nigh on a quarter of a century but none of it would have happened had it not been for Tommy Docherty.

The Doc had, let's just call it a colourful career both as a player and a manager — he walked hand in hand with controversy — and now makes a comfortable living telling sportsman's dinners about the funnier, and often the seamier side of his soccer adventures.

But there was nothing at all funny about Jocky Scott's experience at the hands of the Doc back in 1964. The prescription handed to the teenage Aberdonian was very hard medicine to swallow. And the 'Dear John' letter he received was to all but shatter the confidence of the youngster who appeared to have the soccer world at his feet.

As a 13-year-old attending Aberdeen Grammar School, young Scott was showing enough promise to suggest that he might follow in the footsteps of his father who had played for his home-town Aberdeen and Newcastle United. Jocky was training at Pittodrie — where he first met trainer Teddy Scott, amazingly still on the Dons staff — but like many before him, there was a reluctance to commit himself to his local heroes.

Said Jocky: 'I was asked to sign provisional forms, but as much as I liked Aberdeen, after all I was a keen supporter of the club, I didn't want to sign for them in case I was a failure. And my father thought it best that I started my career away from the glare of my home town.'

By the time Scott had graduated to the Scotland Schoolboys side in 1963 the scouts were knocking at his door.

'Depending on which way you look at it fortunately or unfortunately — I chose Chelsea although Manchester United, Arsenal, Sheffield Wednesday, Bolton, Preston were also interested.

'The Doc signed me on a three-year contract and I played in the youth team, finishing that season as joint top goal-scorer.

'I had gone home for the summer and I got a letter from Chelsea. My father came in with the letter and I thought it would be to inform me when to report back for pre-season training. Unfortunately, when my father opened it and read it he just left it on the end of the bed and walked out of my room — it was to tell me not to come back. Needless to say I was a bit shattered. At that time you are a 15-year-old boy and you go down to London, you believe everything that people are telling you and you sign a contract without really reading anything in it. You just sign it because you are desperate to get into football.

'I can look at it both ways. Unfortunately, I had picked the wrong club because I only lasted a year down there and at a

The teenage Jocky Scott displays his skills.

time when I thought I was doing alright. I could have gone to bigger clubs but fortunately I chose Chelsea because they had just been promoted and I felt that going there would give me more of an opportunity to make a career than if I had gone to bigger clubs like Manchester United or Arsenal, or Rangers who were also wanting me to sign.

'I say fortunately going to Chelsea because after leaving I got picked up by Dundee and ended up having a good career there. Had I gone elsewhere, other than Chelsea, I might have ended up in obscurity . . . you just don't know.'

The Stamford Bridge set-back would have broken lesser boys but Jocky retraced his steps back to Aberdeen Lad's Clubs and tried to disguise his fear that senior football would not give him a second chance.

But very soon Jocky was invited down to Dens to take part in the club's pre-season training. 'During my early days nothing happened because it was just running, running, plodding through the streets of Dundee trying to keep up with Sammy Kean on his bike.' Then Scott got the second chance he craved when Dundee held their public pre-season trial. These games involved signed players and trialists and were well-known for unearthing the odd gem here and there.

One was certainly discovered that night — Jocky Scott was in action throughout the trial — and that meant he was a real good 'un.

'I was fortunate enough to play the three "halves" and fortunate enough as well to score a couple of goals which attracted Bob Shankly to sign me. There was one incident in the trial which I will always remember.

'Bert Slater was in goals and the ball was played through. Bert came running out but I got there first and stuck the ball by him and jumped over his spreadeagled body. And as I was running back towards the centre line Bert stood up and said "You little – – – – –, if you do that again I'll – – – – – break your leg." That was introduction to the type of player, the type of determination that Bert Slater had as a goal-keeper, and the type of attitude you could expect from a hardened pro.'

That night was the Dens Park fans' first introduction to the scurrying, terrier-like style that Scott was to make his own. His appearance often took on that of a reluctant star. He often looked as if he'd wished he'd gone to the pictures and was in the huff because he had to play football. But reluctant star or not, the impression the youngster gave was definitely a false one and what the fans had seen had marked down Scott as one to watch, one for the future.

But little did they know the 'future' was just around the corner. An indifferent start to the League Cup campaign persuaded Shankly to field some of his promising youngsters when Motherwell came to town for a meaningless Wednesday night match on August 26th, 1964.

The youngsters did Shankly and Dundee proud but this, above all, was Jocky Scott's match as the Dark Blues slaughtered the Steelmen.

'He made six changes and I was in alongside other youngsters John Phillips, Alex Totten and Ally Donaldson, and we beat Motherwell 6-0 which was exciting. I didn't score but I felt I did everything but. The main thing was I thoroughly enjoyed it and I showed that I could handle playing in the first team albeit it wasn't to be for long. It was great and that obviously gave me a tremendous lift having three months earlier been sacked by Chelsea . . . that was pleasing.

'Unfortunately, the next game I made a mess of it because I was sent off at Brockville. Falkirk at that time had an Irish internationalist called Sammy Wilson who later became one of my team-mates at Dens. I had the ball and Sammy tackled me from the back and I took exception to this and just stood up and kicked him and I was properly sent off for retaliation. It was a rash and stupid thing to do, but at the time I was annoyed . . . it was one of these rushes of blood to the head that players take and being a young boy, the blood went quicker to the head at that time!'

Before the SFA suspension caught up with him, Scott played half a dozen games in the first team including one which gave him a taste for derby encounters that has not left him to this day. 'We went to Tannadice and beat United 4-1 in front of nearly 20,000 people. Coming from Aberdeen I didn't know anything about the derby scenario and to score twice was brilliant.' One of these goals was a rarity — a header — but Scott denies it almost apologised to keeper Sandy Davie as it trundled towards the corner of the net!

'When I first broke through there was a great quality throughout the team — Hammy and Coxer at full back, Bobby Seith, George Ryden at centre half before they bought Jim Easton from Hibs, Bobby Wishart, Alan Cousin, Hughie Robertson, Andy Penman and then Charlie Cooke arrived to add his abundance of talent to the scene.'

Of course, great deeds in Europe were still commonplace in and around Dens Park. And young Scott was part of it all in season 1967-68 when the Dark Blues again came within touching distance of a European final. This time it was in the Fairs Cup — predecessor of today's UEFA Cup — and teams to crumble to the Dundee skill and fire-power were DWS Amsterdam, Royal Liege, George McLean remarkably scoring all the goals in Dundee's super 4-1 win in Belgium, and FC Zurich.

Then in May 1968, the might of Don Revie's Leeds United were the semi-final opponents and these were two great games between two very evenly matched outfits. Almost 25,000 saw Bobby Wilson on target for Dundee in the 1-1 first-leg draw at Dens and although Dundee matched the Lilywhites at Elland Road a fortnight later, a goal from Eddie Gray gave the pride of Yorkshire the verdict. Scott came in for both matches against Zurich and both against Leeds and that sharpened his awareness of the Continental pedigree of the club.

And there were more adventures to follow, particularly in 1971-72. Akademisk of Copenhagen were dealt with in the first round and then Dundee came back from the dead to beat Cologne after one of the most exciting nights Dens Park has ever seen. Then it was 'deja vu' again as the draw paired John Prentice's Dundee with AC Milan, who had of course beaten the club in the 1962-63 European Cup semi final.

'We played over in the San Siro and we lost 3-0 — big George Stewart doing his normal own goal routine for their first — but even that was one helluva an experience — the crowd, the atmosphere, very frightening. Losing 3-0, most thought we had no chance but we beat them 2-0 at Dens and played them off the park and we were unfortunate not to take it to extra time. And that will always go down as Duncan Lambie's game because he tore them apart and ran riot.'

That was regarded as the kind of tactical masterstroke of which Prentice was always capable. Lambie was known as an out and out winger with phenomenal running power. That

Boss Man . . . Scott as manager at Dens Park.

night at Dens, Prentice switched him to inside forward and he all but destroyed the Italians single-handed through the middle where they least expected it.

Jocky's eyes brighten as he takes up the story of the Dens era when Prentice was in charge with Jim McLean as coach.

'I would have to say that time was possibly the best in the sense that we were fitter, there was a whole new outlook, a new dimension to training. Wee Jim brought new ideas when he became coach, working more on basic skills as well as fitness.

'I think at that time at Dens Park there was a good harmony about the place, players that blended well together, there was more of a professional outlook to the whole scene and more awareness as far as the players were concerned about the jobs they should be doing as a team player rather than being just individuals.

'That was possibly the first time we were introduced to anything like coaching as we know it nowadays. Although we didn't win anything at that time I think that was possibly one of the best teams that I had played in.'

'I can understand that Prentice was very good in terms of tactics, ideas, he could see things, but I felt that the way he spoke about them were away above some of the player's heads because we maybe weren't used to some of the ideas he was putting forward. Whereas Wee Jim helped in that respect because he brought it down to the more basic, laymen's language!

'Together they were a very good partnership. A lot of us were very, very disappointed that Wee Jim didn't take over when John Prentice left to become manager of Scotland but Jim had his own reasons for not staying and we all know what he's done since going across the road.

'The players at the time all had their head turned by Jim. I had played alongside him with Dundee and I knew what he was like on the park, never stopped moaning. He was never looked upon by the Dundee public as being one of the best but he was a fine player with a lot of ablity. He maybe couldn't run that quick but certainly had bags of skill, a good touch, and was a good passer of the ball. But for some unknown reason the Dundee public never really took to him.

'Then when he was appointed coach by John Prentice, first of all I wondered what we were in for. Because Jim had

Perfect . . . Jim McLean scores from the spot against DWS Amsterdam at Dens in the Fairs Cup.

never struck me as being coaching material but, to be fair to the man, after a couple of months working under him, then I had to change my mind and respected everything he did even though it meant, within his time there, you were at the end of a tongue lashing from him.

'But that was his way, always has been, and it's got him results. Even allowing for the fact that Dundee won the League Cup after Jim had left, I would think that it was a bad time for Dundee Football Club when Jim McLean was allowed to leave. He went across the road and transformed United. They were always regarded as underdogs, the second best team in the city, and he has transformed them into being the top team in the town and they have been for many years — if only for the simple reason that they've stayed in the Premier League, they've been in Europe so often, they've played in Cup Finals, both the League Cup and the Scottish Cup. They've won the Premier League Championship — a remarkable achievement.

'The one thing Jim admitted at the time of his departure was that he left very good players at Dens to work with not-so-good players. He would admit that had he stayed at Dens or if he could have taken all the players he wanted to take to Tannadice, I think he would have had a much better team and maybe even more success . . .'

You only have to talk to players who have worked under Jim McLean to realise — reluctantly or otherwise — that the man has something special to offer and you'll gather that Jocky Scott is one of his disciples. Others who have made their mark coaching in the Scottish game are Walter Smith, Archie Knox, Gordon Wallace, Doug Houston, Kenny Cameron, Paul Hegarty and Billy Kirkwood.

And although McLean had moved across the road by the time Dundee won the League Cup in 1973, he was very much in the thoughts of many of the team. Let Jocky explain:

'Not showing any disrespect to Davie White as a manager, when we won the League Cup, we had a reception at the Angus Hotel after the game, for the players and their wives. Six or seven of us chose to leave the reception early and visit Wee Jim. We did that to thank him because we felt it was due to him, what he had done with us in the period he was there, that we'd been able to achieve our League Cup success, winning something at last.

'That was done with no thought of disrespect to coach Harry Davis or Davie White, but we felt we had to pay our debt of gratitude to someody we all thought had done us a great turn.

'Word got back to the manager that this had happened and he was none too pleased about it. I think if you check the records, within three years of that happening, the boys who were culprits of going down to see Wee Jim at his house were no longer at Dens Park.

'I think Jim was touched by the whole thing, him being the manager of your immediate enemies as it were, and us having won the Cup, going down to visit him. We weren't there for very much longer.

Euro Strike . . . Racing White Daring of Belgium are the opposition as Scott gets on the target.

'I think someone had phoned Davie White or he'd heard from one of the other players that we were missing and somebody maybe told him where we'd gone. It wasn't until a couple of weeks later that we were brought in by the manager and disciplined for it. That was the beginning of the end for the players involved. He obviously thought he couldn't trust us again or that we didn't want to be part of what was going on. So one by one we departed the scene.'

The League Cup triumph was Dundee's last domestic honour and Scott nurses fond memories.

'It was my only trophy as a player at Dens Park and what I recall most, other than the fact we won, is that there was a miners' strike and a three-day working week. The game kicked off really early and it was a very bleak December day with no floodlights. It was wet, and dreary and there were only about 28,000 in to watch which I think is the lowest Hampden crowd for a Cup Final.

'We did well, we survived a lot of hairy moments and Gordon scored a great goal. And yes, it was a great feeling going up to collect the Cup. Despite all the problems going against the occasion, it was my first Final and I had been with the club for nine years, and all we thought about was getting out there, enjoying the moment and, of course, winning the trophy.'

The 'Gordon' that Scott refers to almost in the passing needs no introduction. For a huge part of the Jocky Scott success story as a player at Dens was built on the solid foundation of his partnership with Gordon Wallace, now Scott's No. 2 at Dunfermline. They were made for each other — the kind of telepathic partnership that is heaven sent.

'The thing I enjoyed about the time we won the League Cup was that on the park and off it I had a great relationship with Gordon. Right from the start we struck up a great understanding, nothing to do with coaching, just two players getting together as can sometimes happen, players who can read each other and know without thinking what is going to happen.

'For me, Gordon was one of the most under-rated players ever to play for the club. I think it was really only near the end of his time at Dens that he was appreciated for the kind of player he was . . . great to play with, great for building moves and he could score goals too. Gordon and I always used to work little 1-2s — he was always available and he always knew where to go. You can't coach this it's just two players getting together, it all clicks for them and things happen.

'Off the park, too, Gordon and I are the best of pals and that helped. When we played together and everything fell into place up front between us two, I think it helped the rest of the team and it certainly lifted the supporters because they knew that something was likely to happen.'

There were times when it seemed Dundee's name was on the Scottish Cup but it never happened for Jocky Scott.

'I played in what seemed like umpteen semi-finals against Celtic and we always ended up losing. There was no reason for this other than Celtic were a better side — remember we're going back to Jock Stein's days — nine League titles in a row

— and at the time, although they weren't invincible, they seemed to be cleaning up. We just happened to be unfortunate to be drawn against them all the time — and funnily enough the time we won the League Cup was the only occasion we didn't get them at the semi stage . . . and we beat them in the Final.'

There was an epic campaign in season 1973-74. 'We were drawn away to Aberdeen, who a year or two earlier had won the Cup and we went up there on a Sunday and slaughtered them 2-0 — we played them off the park. We were than drawn to play Rangers at Ibrox and again it was a Sunday game. You go to these places as underdogs but we slaughtered Rangers 3-0. We then went to Easter Road to take on Hibs who were a good side at the time. It was 3-3, a great game for the spectators — it must have been terrific to watch. Then in the replay we beat Hibs 3-0 with over 33,000 at Dens.

'We thought this could be our year — this could be the year we avoid Celtic but no such luck. We felt if the draw had been kinder we would have lifted the Cup but once more our Celtic jinx at Hampden struck and they beat Airdrie in the Final.'

The time Jocky knew was coming — when he would be moved on by Davie White — finally happened in August, 1975. 'Although I was still in the team, the writing had been on the wall after what I'd done in the wake of the League Cup triumph. The manager had obviously taken exception to it which he was probably right in doing — but from then on I'd always had the feeling that things wouldn't be the same again and it could happen any time.' And so Scott moved to Pittodrie with Ian Purdie plus £20,000 coming down the A92 in the opposite direction.

It was the first season in the Premier League and one that was to prove disastrous to the Dark Blues. Despite a brave, late surge in which the inspiration of Eric Sinclair — a cult hero to Dens fans — first emerged, Dundee were relegated on goal difference thanks to an unlikely Dundee United win at Ibrox in their last game.

Said Jocky: 'During that season Aberdeen battled against Dundee and Dundee United to avoid the drop. It's ironic that these three teams all ended up with the same points total and one, Dundee, going down on goal difference. The other two have never looked back since.'

Jocky was brought back to Dens Park by then manager Tommy Gemmell after he'd won a second League Cup medal with the Dons. But a back injury which subsequently required surgery limited his playing appearances. 'At that time I had no intention of going into coaching because I just wanted to keep playing for as long as possible. When I had the operation I thought my playing days were over and I actually applied for a few jobs outside football without any success. I was still on a contract at Dens and Willie Wallace had indicated he would be going to Australia which of course meant there was gong to be a vacancy on the coaching staff.

'One day I was lying in bed — I couldn't do any training at the time — and I saw an advert in the paper seeking a reserve coach at Dens. So I applied, had a word with Tam Gemmell and was told a few days later that I could get the job until the end of the season while they had a look to see what I could do.'

When Donald Mackay took over, Scott had managed to attain a higher level of fitness and he was brought back into first-team action. 'I was in for half a dozen games but unfortunately I could never get close to the standard I'd set before and so my comeback was over almost before it started when I was told politely my services as a player were no longer required!'

That might have done Scott a favour as he gradually built on his coaching reputation — so much so that when Mackay left he wanted the manager's job and was deeply hurt when he didn't get it.

'I felt I had done enough and was experienced enough to take over. Fortunately for me the directors thought otherwise and Archie Knox was appointed. I say fortunately because Archie taught me so much in the two years I worked under him.

Scramble . . . Leeds United put their iron curtain at Dens in the Fairs Cup semi-final with Sammy Wilson, Steve Murray and Alex Kinninmonth prominent.

'Eventually, I was glad they had given him the job instead of me because it could quite easily have gone the other way for me and I could have made a mess of it and been out of a job.'

When Knox, his rebuilding job on and off the park having transformed the atmosphere within the club and given the fans so much optimism, left for Aberdeen, Jocky Scott, former player, former reserve team coach, former first team coach and recent assistant manager was finally in the job he craved.

'Being manager was enjoyable and yet frustrating. Frustrating from the point of view of working to an aim which was to get back into Europe again. By the time I took over there were no worries about relegation — these fears had gone — we were never going to be winning the League but there was always the possibility of a Cup run or getting into Europe, and that was our aim.

'My aim was to carry on what Archie had done and to improve on that. Under Archie we had missed out on Europe by goal difference and I think by one point. That was one of the main reasons Archie left because he missed the European involvement he had at Aberdeen and he was frustrated in that he had been involved in Cup wins and League wins at Pittodrie but he felt that all the work he was doing at Dens, there was nothing at the end of it. And to be honest, Archie transformed Dundee. From the little money he had to work with he brought in men like Robert Connor, John Brown, John McCormack, Stuart Rafferty. He gave the whole place a lift and brought in a totally professional outlook, which demanded more from the players and because demands were being made of them, the players were beginning to reap better rewards obviously through winning more games and there was always optimism that we could get into Europe.'

Scott's last season which ended in bitterness started with so much promise. His inspirational buys Keith Wright and Tommy Coyne were banging in the goals, and Europe beckoned as Dundee opened up a handsome lead over main challengers Dundee United. But the demands on the playing staff were taking a toll and Scott pleaded for money to strengthen his squad.

'I told the directors that if I couldn't freshen up the team we wouldn't get into Europe, only to be told that no money would be forthcoming and that I would have to get on with what I had at my disposal. To be fair to the players they gave everything but it wasn't enough and by the season's end we'd slumped to seventh place.'

The fans were angry and frustrated but so too was Jocky. 'My main frustration was that the next season was just going to be the same and taking everything into consideration including one or two personal things which I would rather not enlarge on, I decided to write a letter of resignation. I must admit one of the factors was that Aberdeen didn't have a manager as Ian Porterfield had just left — that was another angle.

'But my departure could have been better. It was sad and it left me angry if the truth is told. I took my letter to the chairman's house and the thing that angered me was that I spent an hour and a half with him trying to explain why I was resigning and never once in that time did he ask me to happen. I can only hope that in the near future things get sorted out and the club can get back on the right road and resurrect themselves to what they once were.'

Scott won a single Scotland cap — scant reward for his contribution and consistency over many seasons. That was against Russia in 1971 and while he believes he should have been honoured more often, Jocky has this to say: 'Obviously Scotland managers felt there were better players than me about and although I thought that I was good enough to represent my country, it's the managers who pick the team. But in saying that, better players than myself over the years have not received any form of international recognition and in that respect I was fortunate to get a cap. I would have liked to have played for Scotland on home soil though, as my parents, my wife and her family never had the opportunity of seeing me in a Scotland jersey.

'I was delighted to be chosen against Russia after coming on as a sub against Denmark in Copenhagen and although we lost 1-0 in Moscow I thought I did well enough to warrant another outing or at least, to be chosen as a squad member.

'But, ironically, the Russia game was Bobby Brown's last as Scotland manager and there was a new man in charge for the next game when we played Belgium at Pittodrie, and old friend of mine from Chelsea, a chap called Tommy Docherty . . .'

ERRATUM
The following paragraphs should read on between pages 146 & 147:

reconsider my position and never once was I told — "You're not going anywhere, you're staying with Dundee." So I left the chairman's house knowing full well that I wasn't wanted. Nothing was really made public, and to this day people ask me about the circumstances of my departure. It wasn't the way I would have liked to have left.

There can be no doubt that it was Scott's wish to leave Dens but there can be little argument either if it is asserted that chairman Angus Cook did little to keep him   if only until the end of his contract. Cook's friendship with Plymouth Argyle manager Dave Smith was known to many and the Dens supremo would often talk in glowing terms of Smith's prowess as a soccer manager.

However, regardless of the circumstances of his departure, Scott looks back at his long association with the club with a fondness that by far outweighs the rancour, 'I enjoyed nearly every minute of my time at Dens. At one time Dundee were the No. 1 club in the city, the best-supported club in the city and the fans had optimism at the start of every season, looking forward to European ties, to Cup runs. All this had gone and I think it's tragic it should

CHAPTER NINE

John Duncan

AS A SCHOOLBOY IN SHORT TROUSERS JOHN Duncan dreamed of banging in match-winning goals for his favourite football team.

And, like so many other schoolboys in Dundee, he watched in wonder as his local heroes brought the League Championship to the city for the first time in history.

In particular, he was open-mouthed in awe and admiration at two men in particular in that Grand Old team — Alan Gilzean and Andy Penman, two men who would play a major role as John Duncan's soccer story unfolded.

The famous names of that era are, of course, currently immortalised in the 'Up wi the Bonnets' rendition that greets the Dark Blues to this day as they take the field.

The song rolls easily off the tongues of today's small boys who relate to these heroes of old through tales told by their fathers and grandfathers. And to that famous old tune, it goes like this:

'There was Robertson, Penman and Alan Gilzean. With Smith there and Cousin the finest you've seen. A defence that is steady, heroic and sure, Liney, Hamilton, Cox, Seith and Wishart and Ure.'

Sadly the words now too often echo round more empty spaces than supporters, but they serve as a fond reminder of once-proud days that might, one day not too far distant, be repeated.

148

We've done it . . . George Stewart celebrates at Hampden with John Duncan.

When Dundee won the flag and embarked on their great European Cup adventure John Duncan was knee high to a crush barrier behind the Provost Road goal. And he had very few thoughts in his mind other than the prospect of pulling a Dark Blue jersey over his head.

Sometimes dreams come true and they certainly did for Duncan. Within four years of seeing the Championship won, the tall, square-shouldered 16-year-old was sharing a dressing room with Penman. And the first time he rose unguarded at the back post to powerfully head home in a Dens Park practice match, he was given a nickname that follows him to this day — and incidentally a nickname that he carries with pride. It was George Stewart who thought it up and they called him Gillie.

Big George was good with nicknames but perhaps he had a crystal ball — for this Gillie the Second was later to follow his boyhood hero down the big-money road to London and Tottenham Hotspur.

The young Duncan at Clepington Road Primary School and later Morgan Academy was set on playing football for Dundee.

But his early impact as a primary player was less than sensational. 'Although I had no trouble getting a game for my school team there was no question of representative honours although like many youngsters, I did manage to get trials for Dundee Schoolboys.

'But to be honest, at that stage, I was far more interested in watching Dundee and I went to Dens Park every chance I got. It was my grandfather who took me, we would meet at the corner of Tannadice Street and Provost Road and when I was really young, I would go and see Dundee "A" — he wouldn't take me to see the big matches until I was a bit older — and I recall seeing Alan Gilzean playing with the reserves although he never struck me at the time as being exceptional.

'I didn't get to see the first team until I was about seven or eight and my earliest memories were of players like George McGeachie, Davie Sneddon and George Merchant. When we won the League I was fortunate enough to see most of the home games and many of the away matches too.

'Gilzean and Penman were my favourites and although Alan had been unexceptional in the reserves, once he made it into the team he was absolutely outstanding.'

Duncan was typical of a schoolboy from that era — he and his pals went to Tannadice back and forward but the Dark Blues were the top notchers and he never thought about any other team.

By the time he went on to Morgan Academy — where as luck would have it Duncan had to concentrate on the oval ball — the youngster was beginning to show some promise at soccer.

Butterburn Boys Club were the top-dog under-age team and young Duncan proceeded to force his services on them.

'I didn't give them the chance to pick me — I was that keen. I was so desperate to play football that I approached them for a game long before I was old enough to play. I lived in Barnes Avenue, just around the corner from Graham Street Park where they played and I just became part of the scenery. I would turn up every week trying to get a game and desperately hoping that not enough players would turn up.

'I played occasionally but my outings were few and far between. Nevertheless I trained with them twice a week and that meant when I did eventually become old enough to play they knew enough about me and knew what I could do.

'At schoolboy level I got into the Dundee Under-15 side and also the last 44 for a place in the Scotland team but no further.

'I wasn't particularly academic and eventually I was persuaded that it would be a good idea to go to Jordanhill and let's just say I did enough at school to get there. But still I had my heart set on being a player. I know it sounds funny but it never entered my head that I was going to be anything different.

'At the time I never realised how lucky I was to come through it all and I know nearly every young lad wants to be a football star but I was very lucky to get the opportunity and very fortunate that I was given every encouragement at home.

'My dad would go out to see me in all the games I played in and he even kept that up as much as he could when I came down to England. I had that sort of help from home all the time and it made a big difference.'

It was while playing for Butterburn that Duncan first came to the notice of the senior scouts and a man called Andy Irvine, who played in the Scottish Cup Final for Falkirk in 1957 and spent many years as a player at Dens Park, was scouting for Dark Blue manager Bobby Ancell. 'I knew his son quite well, he was called Andy too, and was at the Morgan with me. I think he recommended me to his father and Mr Irvine watched me quite a few times until I eventually signed Schoolboy forms for Dundee in April 1966 at the age of 16. By then I was training one night at Butterburn and one night with Dundee with the other youngsters.

'For me this was the big time, it was Dens Park and Dundee Football Club and that was all I had ever wanted, I just wanted to be one of the stars. Andy Penman was still at the club but there were other big names, George McLean, Alex Stuart, Jim McLean, Jocky Scott.'

Despite his obvious determination to make it as a footballer, Duncan received good advice from home and covered his options by staying on at school and completing his studies with a view to going on to PE College at Jordanhill. 'I was still as keen as ever to be a footballer but I must admit the advice I got from home to get something else behind me was totally correct.' It was O levels and Highers during the day and his educational thoughts turned to all things football at night. The next stage for Duncan was to get a game with the reserves to show what he could do. 'I was desperate for the phone call from the club saying that I was in and eventually that happened. It may be through planning by the management or it may happen because of injuries but whatever it was I remember getting the call to play at Dens against Dundee United Reserves and I scored with a header as we beat them 3-2. Nothing much happened after that but at the start of the next season there was another phone call and I was in at Aberdeen against the reserves and I scored in that one as well. After that I was offered a part-time contract for a year. I was of course still at school, in sixth year, and I recall the papers made quite a big thing about the schoolboy footballer.'

'Two other local lads who signed at that time were Brian Knight and Mitchell Goodall who were Dundee boys like me and they were signed on part-time contracts although fairly soon they had packed in school and gone full-time. But they were only at Dens for a couple of years and in a way it

Such drama . . . Dundee's Bobby Wilson and John Duncan pile on the pressure against Cologne in the attack leading up to the Dundee winner.

underlined the wisdom of the advice I got. I think Mitch emigrated to New Zealand and Brian is now living down in Northampton.'

Duncan was grateful for the advice given to him by Bobby Ancell and Bobby Seith who was coaching at Dens. 'Ancell had signed me and I always found him a great source of encouragement, I always got the feeling he thought I had talent and that I was going to be alright. Bobby Seith was good to me as well and I only have good memories of the way I was treated during my early days. At that time Seith was involved mainly with the first team but he still made time to spend hours with me, remember I was only a young boy, but I always remember that both of them spent time with me when they had more important things to do. An awful lot of coaching is making a player think he is really good and that goes a long long way to helping his game and that is how it worked for me.'

When Duncan achieved his target by going to Jordanhill College he found things a bit more difficult than he first thought it would be. 'Being a footballer and studying to be a PE teacher sounds compatible although in reality it was not like that. The reason is that we were doing physical stuff at college all week and to be honest I think that held me back

153

from making the real breakthrough into the first team. In my early years at Dens I would be able to get into the team at the start of the season but when I went back to college I seemed to drop out of the picture. It was a combination of the hard work at college and the fact that being a part-timer I would miss training and tactics talks during the week. At Jordanhill we often worked very hard on Fridays and this was not good if you were meant to be playing the next day. I would find that I was doing hard work at the wrong times. The Principal at Jordanhill was Bomber Brown — he was very good with players and there were quite a few of them at Jordanhill, Bobby Clark, Andy Roxburgh, there was a kind of football tradition there.'

Ancell was still in charge when Duncan first broke through to first team action. In season 1968/69 he was in the team from the start and played through into October scoring eight goals — a statistic that backs up his Jordanhill theory. Then, his college course complete and his qualification stored away for the future, Duncan went to see Ancell's successor, John Prentice, and asked for a full-time contract. He got it.

At this time Duncan felt he should have been in the team more often than he was. 'I felt I was scoring goals when I did play but because of the system John Prentice used I was not always involved. It seemed the only way I would get in was on the wing and I was happy to do that and of course I scored a lot of goals from there. Perhaps it was the right thing for me because I still wasn't that strong, I was a late developer. Playing wide taught me the game and many people were of the opinion that I should stay there. I scored goals from the right but I wanted to get into the box and be a striker.

'If John Prentice was an occasional critic of my team contribution, he was probably right — my one thought was to score. Okay, I wasn't totally out for myself, I didn't dribble and try to beat people just to get a scoring chance, but if I felt there was an opportunity I would have a go. I was definitely the single-minded type who wanted to score goals and although I

Johnny on the spot . . . Duncan beats the Milan defence to score in the UEFA Cup-tie at Dens.

can't disagree with Prentice's assessment he did pick me in a responsible position for a young player. I had to cover the left back making forward runs and that was a responsibility.

'I don't think I particularly suited his style as a front player, because he played it basically with one up, Gordon Wallace. Gordon was a fine player and at that time a lot better at playing the kind of game Prentice wanted. He had vast experience and was superb at holding the ball up and bringing others into the game. When I was older I thought I could do that job just as well if not better but at the time I think Prentice was right.'

It was during the Prentice reign that Duncan enjoyed one of his finest hours as a Dark Blue it was the night Cologne revisited Dens Park in the UEFA Cup with a 2-1 first leg lead. Oh what a night, November 3, 1971.

'It was a tremendous night and I still have a vivid memory of the way it unfolded. Quite early on we won a corner on the right and I got my head on the end of it from quite far out but my direction was good and the ball flew into the net at the postage stamp corner. But then Cologne came into the game and they scored two goals which put them 2-1 up on the night and 4-2 ahead on aggregate.

'It looked like a lost cause but we kept battling away and with about 20 minutes to go I got my second. A Jim Steele cross from the left, I chested it down and wheeled to beat their keeper. Then we were back in front when I scored from quite close in and by that time the pressure we had on the German goal was quite frantic. In the dying minutes a long ball was played into the box and I went up to challenge the keeper for it and the ball broke loose.

'Gordon went for it and his shot was blocked on the line by what seemed a hand ball. We were all appealing for a penalty when Bobby Wilson followed up and rammed home the winner from close range. It was amazing — I think everybody bar our keeper was in the box and when the ball went in the players and the crowd went daft.'

Such was the excitement of the moment — remember the Germans were a crack outfit and they'd been two goals clear as the match entered its closing stages — that the BBC camerman nearly missed the magic moment. In fact he probably did but surely we can forgive him. It was a night of great emotions — some of the German players were in tears — and Duncan was the toast of the terraces.

'John Prentice wasn't an emotional man but believe me, he was that night. He'd thrown me up front to get goals and he told me in the dressing room — "You've shown what you can do. Use this as a launch pad and go on from here." '

That was a preface to yet another old foe from the European arena returning to Dens. In the next round it was AC Milan and they came with a seemingly comfortable lead from the San Siro Stadium. Gordon Wallace scored early for Dundee and Duncan made it 2-0 but time ran out and it was so close and yet so far. 'Duncan Lambie was outstanding for the club that night he was in the game all the time and even managed to hit the post when we were looking for an equaliser. AC Milan used man for man marking and it was a masterstroke by Prentice to use Duncan Lambie as a runner, he could take the ball past people at ease and that night he was different class.'

The following season was the one that Duncan took off in scoring terms. On the opening day he hit five against lowly East Stirlingshire to serve notice that he was the man to finish off Dundee's good football and translate all their fine outfield play into goals.

'That was a memorable season. I scored 40 times in domestic matches and twice for the Scottish League against the English League at Hampden and was Scotland's top goalscorer. My feeling then was that everything I was trying was coming off. Gordon Wallace played well, too, and he created a lot for me. Apart from my five at East Stirling I scored a hattrick against Partick Thistle and then I managed four in the Scottish Cup match at Stranraer.'

Duncan's name and reputation was gaining in status all the time and scouts from down south were beginning to pay attention. And he certainly did his image no harm at all with two goals that gave the Scottish League a 2-2 draw at Hampden. 'Alan Gordon of Hibs was injured and I was called in by Willie Ormond. I remember I had a calf strain on the Saturday before but I was not going to tell anyone because I really wanted to play. I remember England scored early on and we were supposed to be slaughtered because they had their best team out which was almost a full international team. Peter Shilton, Mick Mills, David Nish, Roy McFarland, Mick Channon, Frank Worthington, they were all good players and it was going to be a tough game. But then I recall Derek Johnstone, who was playing centre half, broke into the box from deep and the ball came over his shoulder, hit him and bounced into the box. I did what I know best — I reacted quickly and hit it with my right foot and although Shilton got a touch he could not stop it going in. Ten minutes later Tommy McLean got the ball 30 yards out. I made a run to the near post, and Tommy chipped it right onto my head and I nodded it home. I remember the goals vividly. England equalised later on but it was a big night for me and I don't think I could have played any better than I did that night. Derek Parlane played up front beside me and he did an amazing amount of running which suited me and I thought it would have been a good combination had they picked us for Scotland but it did not work out that way.

'Big clubs were sniffing around and as much as Dundee was my team, always has been and always will be, the lure of going down and playing in the English First Division was something I wanted. I needed to prove I could do it but I had to wait despite my good performance at Hampden. I never got a full cap but there were a lot of good players around at that time, although I think I deserved one.'

Duncan believes one of his best games for the club was the December day in 1973 when they beat Celtic 1-0 to win the League Cup, the last domestic trophy to come to Dens Park. 'Although I did not score that day I did well. Gordon scored the goal, it was a lovely effort but manager Davie White must take some of the credit for our success. He withdrew me a bit back from Billy McNeill in between midfield and Gordon, and Jocky played on the right whereas previously it would have been Gordon and I up front. I saw at lot of the ball that day and did well as a creative player passing and making things happen. Gordon's goal was fit to win any cup, it was a really super effort. It was my first final and all I was interesting in doing was playing. I remember on the bus going through I wondered how I would cope and it gave me a bit of belief that I knew that on the day I could do it and that gave me a lot of confidence.'

That success in winning a trophy at Hampden inspired one and all at Dens Park and there was a belief about the place that great things could be around the corner. And the amazing

What a goal . . . Celtic's Ally Hunter can't get to Gordon Wallace's League Cup winner.

Scottish Cup run that followed surely added to that opinion. It was all to end in tears in the by-then customary semi-final meeting with Celtic at Hampden but earlier rounds suggested that there was only one name on the Scottish Cup and that was Dundee's.

The third round draw paired Dundee with Aberdeen at Pittodrie and the A92 going north was a solid mass of traffic that Sunday as Dundee's cup adventure began. Jim Henry scored an own goal although Dave Johnstone's shot from 25 yards looked good before the ex-Dundee United player put a deflection on it and a second from Robert Robinson put Dundee's name into the hat for Round Four.

And that was another tough 'un — this time it was Rangers at Ibrox and again it was a Sunday tie. The soccer played that day by the men in white from Dens Park came from another planet and the Ibrox legions could hardly believe it as Dundee won comfortably 3-0 with goals from Jocky Scott and two from John Duncan. Then in Round Five with some lesser lights still in the competition and Dundee perhaps thinking they were due a wee rub of the green, the draw was again a bit unkind. This time it was Hibs at Edinburgh and what a thriller it turned out to be. Jocky Scott, Jimmy Wilson and Duncan were again on target for the Dens men in a humdinger of a tie against a Hibs side at the time vying for star billing at the top of the Scottish pile. And so it was on to a Wednesday night replay at Dens Park with more than 33,000 in the ground. Hibs were left without a whisper. Scott, Duncan and Bobby Wilson made it 3-0 and the Dark Blues were in the semi-finals, to face Celtic at Hampden.

Characteristic of these meetings was the man-to-man tussle, very often fought in the air, between Duncan and Billy McNeill and Celtic won that night with McNeill's physical presence dominating and refusing to yield an inch of space to the more skilful Duncan. 'Remember not long before we had beaten them at Hampden in the League Cup Final and so it was disappointing to lose 1-0 because at the time I thought we were the best team in the League. We had beaten Celtic at Parkhead earlier, we had beaten Rangers at Ibrox, Aberdeen at Pittodrie, we had slaughtered Hibs after drawing, we had won the League Cup. It was largely the same team all the time.

'Thomson Allan in goal, the full backs Bobby Wilson and Tommy Gemmell, George Stewart and Iain Phillip in the centre of defence, Jimmy Wilson, Bobby Ford, Bobby Robinson, Duncan Lambie on the left, Jocky Scott, Gordon Wallace. There were some players in that lot.'

A characteristic of Duncan's game apart from his heading prowess was the cute way he scored goals, steering the ball an inch past a goalkeeper's outstretched hand, as if it was guided by a laser beam. 'I had reasonable power in both feet but I never thought you would score any more goals by hitting powerful ones, my plan was to control the ball turn, and get my shot in before the keeper was ready. It never needed to be far away from him if it was right in the corner. I was a penalty box goal scorer and there were not that many scored from outside, hit them early, that was my motto and most of my goals were probably one touch or two touch finishes. My main thought was not to put it over the bar and I always believed that if it was on target it would go in unless the keeper saved it. I reckoned I

scored goals on technique and positional play and that was
something I used to work hard at.'

John Duncan shares the view that Jim McLean should
have been given the chance to take over at Dens although he
was warm in praise of Prentice's successor Davie White. 'When
Prentice packed in the job should have gone to McLean. We
had the feeling at Dens that he really didn't want to go to
Tannadice but he did because the club gave him no option but
to move and I think it would be fair to say, although it hurts,
that they have paid for that day.'

Duncan's goal scoring exploits and his brief sortie to the
centre stage of attention against the English League at
Hampden had sent him thinking that the grass might be greener
south of the border. 'I started to look elsewhere and the money
seemed better but there was no freedom of contract so all
players were tied without any right to negotiate. Nowadays, the
better players get the better money but it didn't happen so I had
to look to move. There was a lot of talk of me going to Rangers
and then Celtic were reported to have made a £50,000 bid for
me and that did not help my situation. Davie White was very
fair, he wanted to hang on to me but I wanted to go and play in
England and unfortunately it was not down to him how much
money the club was going to give me and although I was a
Dundee boy through and through I felt I was not getting a fair
deal. In any other job or occupation, if you did not like the
terms you would go and get another job if you were good
enough to move and I felt at that time I was good enough but I
couldn't do it because Dundee had control of my destiny.

'So I went in and said, look, unless you give me a new
contract or let me go I'm off. At that time I did get a good
contract out of it, a decent contract at the beginning of that
very good season when we won the League Cup. At that time I
did not think Dundee were good payers. Everybody always
wants more and there was a little bit of unhappiness which was
sorted out and I think all the lads got a bit more if I remember
correctly.

'Eventually I became unsettled again and Davie White agreed that it was right that I should go. They decided they would not let me go until they got a replacement. It was then they signed Bobby Hutchison from Montrose but I still did not get away and I was beginning to wonder what was going on. I don't hold grudges because it was circumstances that made it hard. Davie White said I was one of his better players and he did not want me to go. I knew I was being hard to deal with but I was determined to do the best for myself and I wanted to see how good I would be in the English First Division.'

And so the day dawned when John Duncan received a phone call from White — the manager had finally given in and the striker was on his way. 'Davie said to me on the phone there is a team at the bottom of the league and they wanted to sign me, so I went down the town, I had my jeans on, picked up the chairman and off we went to meet this club. On the way he told me it was Spurs. I signed in a hotel near Edinburgh Airport and yes they were in fact bottom of the league. Funnily enough, before I put pen to paper I was wondering if it was the right thing to do. Dundee had always been my club and they always have been ever since and I had made my mind up that it had to be done. I was Terry Neill's first signing at Spurs, we had a tough time to begin with but I scored a few goals and we stayed up and in the next season we did really well and I managed 20 odd goals in the First Division which was a lot in these days and that proved to myself that I could play at that level. I used to see the real Gillie occasionally and have a good chat. He would tell me what he thought of how I was doing, we knew each other well and got on super. He would come round to the club and we would bump into each other for a blether. He was a house-hold name down there, a superb player and his reputation went before him all the time.'

Duncan's next move was to Derby County, in a £170,000 deal, but injury to his Achilles tendon and a back problem that meant two operations, brought his playing days to an end. After that his career took him to management at Scunthorpe. 'I

In full flight . . . Duncan bears in on goal.

thought I knew everything there was to know about football and within six months of being a manager I realised I knew nothing' and afterwards he moved to Hartlepool and then Chesterfield and then Ipswich where he spent three season trying to remove the Suffolk club from the English Second Division back into the top flight.

There are some statistics surrounding the player that will upset him as much as it will Dundee fans as they reflect on the time of his £150,000 departure to London. The club's decline was already underway and Duncan, who scored 62 goals in 121 games for the club, was involved in bringing the last domestic honour to Dens Park. He also played and scored in the club's last European game — against Belgian's Racing White Daring of Molenbeek.

His was by no means the last of the big-money departures but he serves as proof — as if any were needed, that a club can't consistently sell its best players and hope to do well.

But Duncan shares the hope that the Dark Blues will come again and he cherishes the memories he has. 'When I was on the terracing I just wanted to be on the park, playing for the club and scoring goals. And I did it — I'll always be proud of that.'

CHAPTER TEN

Jim Duffy

THE SIGHT THAT GREETED HOME FANS AT DENS Park on that very bright but stormy day of March 3, 1990 was one for sore eyes. For the Dundee faithful had come to watch a walking miracle . . . no, much more than that, a miracle who could sprint, tackle and inspire all around him.

Jim Duffy, loved by most in the Dens stands and terracings and respected by all, was back in the Dark Blue jersey to add his considerable presence to Dundee's brave battle for Premier League survival. It was a struggle that was fated not to succeed but Duffy injected hope where there was little and it became a better and more spirited fight thanks to his re-appearance.

Doubtless there were tears shed at Dens that day as the man the fans called Duff faced up to the might of Champions-elect Rangers. There was joy, too, as Dundee grabbed a worthy 2-2 draw in their best performance for weeks.

It was as if Duffy had never been away . . . as if the cruel injury that seemed to have ended his career as a player back in September 5, 1987, had never happened.

There he was, some two and a half years on, back in the heart of the Dundee defence. Said Duffy: 'My only real feeling in that game was a determination not to make any obvious mistakes. I wasn't out to show everybody I could still play, I just wanted to avoid giving away a penalty or making a short pass back. I was concerned that if that happened people would say "he's past it — he's not going to do — the old Jim Duffy wouldn't have done that." '

But then Duffy laughs and scoffs at himself: 'Of course that was nonsense — the pre-injury Jim Duffy was perfectly capable of that kind of blunder. While at my peak, there had been plenty of short pass backs and I'd given away my share of penalties. But that day I knew all eyes were on my every move and I was just trying to get through the 90 minutes without doing anything silly.'

'The team played well and we were a bit unfortunate not to win and once again the Dundee support really helped me.'

For Dundee, entrenched at the bottom since autumn, Duffy's re-appearance as a player was akin to a last throw of the dice but the throw nearly produced a double six as the club's relegation rivals were at last given something to worry about.

Duffy's arrival prompted a mammoth effort to beat the drop and the following Saturday, Dunfermline were victims of a magnificent 35-yarder from Billy Dodds, then Dundee United tumbled 2-1 in a Tannadice derby, thanks to Rab Shannon's magnificent free-kick winner and a backs-to-the-wall second half show with you-know-who directing operations.

Then it was 1-1 at home to Aberdeen followed by a brave point in a goalless game at Tynecastle. All these results had St Mirren and Dunfermline looking over their shoulders.

Duffy played an immense role. 'People say that I nearly worked the miracle for Dundee but that's not the way I saw it. The team had started to play a bit better by the time I arrived without really getting any results. Most had regarded Dundee as being guaranteed relegated and there is always a lifting of pressure when a side has nothing to lose.

'Dundee had been written off from about Christmas and the lads had put that to the back of their mind and started to play a bit. I would say that off the park the atmosphere changed a wee bit and the lads were starting to enjoy their

Stateside . . . Jim Duffy on tour in the States is chased by America's Roy Wegerle who later made a big name for himself in English football.

football a bit more. Maybe me being on the park and being able to organise things helped but big Willie Jamieson had been bought and he made a big difference so it really was an accumulation of things.

'We ended up losing against St Mirren at Dens in a game that really didn't go our way, being a goal ahead right from the kick-off and then missing a penalty. It was a game I should never have played in because I had damaged a hamstring muscle two weeks before and I was never fit. I suppose I conned the manager a wee bit because I was desperate to do my bit. I'd missed that many games before and it was really important for the club and so I wanted to play.

'I got through the 90 minutes but could only play at half pace and that made it difficult for the team. The 2-1 defeat that day made relegation a certainty but I still enjoyed being part of the club again. My legs were maybe not as strong as they should have been but looking to the future, I felt once I'd done pre-season training and reached full fitness I would be a much better player for the club.'

The Duffy fairytale had no happy ending for the Dens Park support in terms of relegation but his presence had given everyone a massive lift . . . and reminded one and all just what they'd been missing in the spell he was out of the game as a player.

If ever a man was meant for a club — it was Jim Duffy for Dundee FC — but it would never have happened but for the determination of Archie Knox, arguably the club's best manager since Bob Shankly.

Duffy's reputation in the game was blossoming even though he'd been rejected by Celtic boss Billy McNeill and had been the mainstay of a Morton defence that had not long conceded more than 100 goals. Knox could pick a winner, bringing the like of Robert Connor and John Brown to Dens Park where they became quality Premier League performers and Duffy, that season's Player of the Year, was another in that mould.

'I believe Paul McStay and Davie Cooper were in the frame for the award and for me, just to be quoted in the same breath, was a great honour. When I actually won I felt that maybe people realised that despite Morton being relegated and despite all the goals that were lost, I never, ever gave up in any game. I gave 100 per cent all the time and I think that maybe the players appreciated that I always tried my best no matter how bad results were. I was still trying to organise things with a lot of young players who had been brought in as well as playing my own game and never letting my head go down and I think that was appreciated.'

Duffy had proved at Morton that he could play in the Premier League and his star-billing amongst the Cappielow faithful repaid manager Benny Rooney's faith in prising Duffy away from reserve team football at Celtic.

'There were an awful lot of good players in the Parkhead second team — Charlie Nicholas, Willie McStay, Danny Crainie, Mark Reid, Pat Bonner — and they all played for the first team. All but one — and that was me. It will probably show in the record books I did have first team outings in, for instance, the Glasgow Cup but as far as I was concerned these did not count.'

Duffy still had faith in his own ability and when the chance came to move to Greenock there was still a part of him that said "Don't go, stay at Celtic and fight for your place." 'My first thought was that I wanted to stay — I still thought I could get a chance — but I was 22 when I left and in football terms that's not young. After all, Paul McStay had about 30 caps by that age.

'Despite what many people think, I never ever felt I had anything to prove to Celtic and my experience there never ever dented my confidence. Really, the only thing you have to prove in football is to yourself and I wanted to prove that I could play in the Premier League. Obviously, I wanted to repay Benny Rooney's faith in me, after all, £20,000 for a reserve was quite a lot for Morton to pay and, for myself, I wanted to find out if I could compete against top quality opposition.

'When my move came, I had been desperate to go for about a year and a couple of clubs had shown a bit of interest. One who talked to me about my future was Alex Ferguson and he said he felt I was a good player and that he had considered me for Aberdeen. He told me I would definitely get my move but he didn't think I would be content being a squad player at Aberdeen which would obviously have been the case with guys like Alex McLeish and Willie Miller about. Fergie was right because I definitely wanted first team football wherever I went but I reckon he knew that a good friend of his, Archie Knox, was interested, and I think that was his way of telling me.

'When my time came to decide, it was between Hibs and Dundee. Hibs weren't prepared to go to a tribunal but Archie was adamant that he wanted me at Dens Park, tribunal or not. That was the difference — Archie's determination although at the time I regarded Hibs as a bigger club.

'I had played for Morton at Dens near the end of the season and I saw that since Knox had gone there, Dundee had become an incredibly hard team to play against, working very hard for each other and definitely looking as if they were on the way up.'

Knox took Duffy up for talks and he made it very difficult for the player to get back home without a commitment that he would pledge his future to the Dark Blues. 'I was prepared to hear what was on offer and go back home to think about it. But Archie wanted the deal settled there and then and he had the Board of Directors at Dens. As we sorted out terms bit by bit he would dodge back and forward to the directors. He was determined and backed me into a corner until he got it. His determination was impressive and so that night I drove back to Glasgow really quite happy at having agreed to sign.

'When I joined for pre-season training I discovered the atmosphere within the club was really great — but I couldn't believe how unfit I was compared to the players. They had all told me how hard Archie's training was but I did not really realise it until I went there. From being part-time to going full-time, I found it very difficult to start with, but the atmosphere was good, the boys were great and it was a great place to be. There was a definite air of confidence about the place.

'Everything seemed to be going well and a lot of that was down to Archie because although he had the reputation of being a hard man, he was great in the training area, getting team spirit to a peak and using a bit of humour into the bargain although he would obviously clamp down hard when he felt it was necessary. The whole thing was very professional.

'By the time the football had started I still didn't think I was as fit as I should have been and when we went on a pre-season tour to Germany, I quickly discovered the other side of Archie — that most people know about.

'He was a man very short on patience in terms of asking you to do a job. If he does not think you are doing it then he is not going to stand about and let you get there gently. He is going to tell you exactly what he thinks of you. One of my first games on tour was against an amateur side — which we won

Proud as punch . . . Jim Duffy with another Player-of-the-Year award won in his time at Dens Park.

quite comfortably. Then we played our second game and John McCormack wasn't playing so Archie made me captain, which came as a big surprise to me although I was very happy.

'But after, he told me he wanted a leader and he said I couldn't lead the Boy Scouts. He told me I was not at Morton any more and I was expected to do a lot better. This happened at a time when I was just getting to know the boys and trying to find my feet and I felt perhaps Archie would have given me a wee bit more time, but he wanted immediate performance and immediate results. It is then you see the other side of the man and start to maybe dislike him a wee bit, but these are things that most players go through and the one thing about Archie is that he never holds grudges. If you could handle the demands he made on you, you could handle anything.

'Back home, Archie wanted me to play a kind of flat back four when I had always been a sort of sweeper type and I felt balls were going over my head and I was getting caught in positions I did not normally find myself in. I felt I wasn't doing anybody any favours — the team or myself. Archie was letting me know. He was telling me I was money down the drain, money he had spent and I was finding all this very difficult.

'But through all this, the Dundee supporters were absolutely unbelievable, I know it sounds patronising but they really were and I think the supporters know that for themselves just how good they were to me. They gave me no stick at all which was strange but really good.

'They gave me the time I needed and I felt that was really, really helpful. I know I was not playing well but I also knew I was not really playing in the way I would like to play.'

The domestic season hadn't long started when Duffy's suspicions that he might be in a bit of bother with his new club were confirmed when he was substituted against Dundee United. That hurt and there was no easing of the pain when the player went knocking on the manager's door. 'You could always talk to Archie — that was no problem — but he started to ask me if I could play in any other position. When that happens you know you've got problems, you very quickly realise you're not doing the job he wants. And it was at that time I honestly thought it was going to be a very short stay for me at Dens Park. I was thinking, I'm not going to be able to fit in and I'll be moving on.'

But the outlook was brighter for Duffy quicker than later.

And the turning point that secured his career under Knox was a game against Motherwell at Fir Park. 'I played well and we had a good result. By that time I was playing more or less the way I preferred — playing my own game which is dropping off either Bobby Glennie or Jimmy Smith — and I felt everyone benefited.

'Looking back, I'd probably been trying too hard to please the manager. He was new to me, very strong-willed and I'd probably been trying to follow his instructions to the letter. He more or less gave me my head, he wasn't backing down but he said he wanted me to play a bit more naturally and while you had to play to the team pattern, Archie gave you a wee bit of freedom so that your strengths could shine through.'

Duffy still wasn't happy with his fitness and he would be back regularly to do extra work. Knox saw him and summoned him. Duffy explained he was doing the extra because he felt short on stamina but Knox said no, and explained that his legs were adjusting back to full-time football and instead of doing extra he should in fact be taking a rest. Knox was right, his rest cure worked and very soon Duffy was a crowd favourite.

'By then the support were showing that they were really getting behind me — I could just sense it. I knew if I brought the ball down, made a good pass or an interception they would cheer or chant my name. And when I met supporters in the town they'd be friendly and warm in their praise. My wife got this too — everyone was very friendly — and all these things made us feel part of the city and helped us settle in so easily.'

The season which had started indifferently, warmed up at the turn of the year and Aberdeen were extremely fortunate to win a Scottish Cup replay at Pittodrie after scraping a 2-2 draw at Dens Park.

'Round about December we went on a really good run and I believe only the arrival of Graeme Souness at Ibrox in April gave Rangers that little boost that got them into Europe ahead of us. We missed out on the last day and that was one of the saddest days of my football career.'

It's a measure of the man that Duffy's disappointment had as much to do with the nightmare Hearts suffered as the League Championship slipped from their grasp. 'We beat them 2-0 and Celtic won at Paisley in one of the most dramatic finales there has ever been. But for me, that was a terrible day. I didn't enjoy it one bit. Naturally, we wanted to win and hoped that Motherwell would get a point at Ibrox. Hearts had been doing so well for so long — they could lose and still finish top — but at time up, we won, Rangers won, and Hearts didn't make it so there were no winners at Dens that day and it made for a very damp atmosphere.'

The man who grabbed the headlines and so scunnered the Jam Tarts was substitute Albert Kidd who came on and grabbed both goals. 'Albert got letters from Celtic fans thanking him but really, he had one of those spells in a game when he was electric. He was always capable but maybe didn't do it often enough. But what about his second goal? It was a fabulous goal and must have ranked alongside the season's best.

'Although we were desperate to win it had absolutely nothing to do with wishing to thwart Hearts. But with only 15 minutes left a buzz went round the Dundee support. Word was that there had been a goal for Motherwell which would have made it 1-1 at Ibrox — but in actual fact it was a penalty for Rangers and that made it 2-0. But the rumour — and yes it was transmitted to the players — meant that the onus was really on us to get a goal which we thought would get us into the UEFA Cup. Hearts were showing a lot of nerves and it looked like they were settling for a point. We definitely sensed it and the roars from our crowd told us that something had happened at Ibrox. That added to the frenzy and we definitely thought we were in Europe.'

But Duffy's joy was short-lived when the truth emerged. 'Afterwards some of the Hearts lads came into the tea room and they were devastated — it was like there had been a death in the family — this unbelievably horrible atmosphere. It was

The crunch . . . Duffy gets in about Brian McClair against Celtic at Parkhead as John Brown awaits the outcome.

agonisingly close and they may never get that close again. I really felt for the players but there were no words you could use to console them — anything would have sounded patronising.

'It was actually quite brave of them to show face and I don't think I would have been so brave. I would have been the first onto the bus saying let's get away from here, let's get down the road. But to their credit, they came in and put a brave face on it but I couldn't help feeling so sorry for them and their supporters.

'We always felt we had to go and win the game and if anyone wanted to criticise, they should perhaps look at the St Mirren aspect because they lost 5-0 and if it had been only 2-0 or something Hearts would still have won on goal difference.'

That close season brought further disappointment for Dundee fans when Archie Knox moved back to Pittodrie although there was satisfaction that Jocky Scott had at long last been given his chance.

'Disappointed as I was to see the club lose Archie, I was pleased Jocky was in, he knew the players and I felt he was a good choice and that turned out to be so. Jocky was a different type — much more reserved in his manner, certainly not as volatile or as exciteable although he learned to be that was as the time passed as most managers do!'

'He did well for the club although I felt he wasn't given the resources to bring in his own players. Like most Dundee managers he had to sell some of the better players — Robert Connor, Ray Stephen, John Brown — but you can't replace men of that quality with guys who maybe cost £30,000 or £40,000. I felt we were losing quality without having the money to buy adequate replacements. Business wise, selling Robert Connor for £300,000 after buying him for a fraction of that might have made sense but, sadly, it was another blow to Dundee supporters and it was a blow for the players too. But these things are outwith your control — you've just got to knuckle down and do the best you can for the club.

'Jocky definitely found a bit of lucky white heather when he signed Tommy Coyne and Keith Wright and they worked brilliantly right from the start. If anyone asked these two I think they would say that Jocky Scott had an awful big say in their success. That's his biggest strength — working with front men, building partnerships because he was a very good player himself in that department. Tommy and Keith are prime examples of what I mean — to score as many goals as they did for a middle-of-the-league side is a great achievement. I believe a lot of that was down to Jocky and Drew Jarvie.'

The highlight of the 1986-87 season was a Scottish Cup run that took Dundee to a Tynecastle semi-final against Dundee United. 'That was another of my big disappointments. It was a great game, a great advert for football and for the City of Dundee but I just felt that day we didn't get the little break you need. You'll rarely get a semi-final with as much entertainment as this one and even at 3-2 down Billy Thomson had two unbelievable saves from John Brown free kicks. Everyone agreed that a draw would have been a fair result.'

Duffy was a rock in a Dark Blue jersey a solid, albeit thin-on-top inspiration not just to the fans but to all around him. And his performance and presence didn't go unnoticed and he won an Under-21 Cap against the Republic of Ireland in 1986. 'I must have been the oldest over-age player in world football but it was one of the proudest moments of my life. I captained a Scotland team to victory and that's something I'll never forget and something I never dreamed would happen to me. That gave me a standing in the professional game that I had always tried to achieve, it meant I was quoted.

'And I'll always be grateful to Dundee for giving me that opportunity, that platform to compete with the best. At the time of my injury I was 28 and often people say that's when a player is about to reach his peak. Dundee were looking as if we were about to achieve something and I felt the next two or three years were going to be great for the club and for me.

'Leading up to the following season all the players were looking forward to it because we knew that in the Coyne-Wright partnership we had something that was really special. We felt we were only a couple of players away from really being able to do something. Then came my last game at Dens before my injury, the League Cup quarter-final against United. There were 20,000 in and the crowd created a terrific atmosphere. I remember us not having too much of the game in the first half but after the break we were getting stronger and when we equalised near the end there was only going to be one extra-time winner.

'I remember talking to Jocky about the lift that win had given the players and the supporters and I said I was really looking forward to Ibrox on the Saturday and playing well. It just so happened my injury came at a time when I was feeling very good and really fit. Naturally, I didn't think it was that bad and my big worry at the time was that I would miss the League Cup semi against Aberdeen. When the consultant advised me I wouldn't be able to play professionally again I was devastated and most people know I shed a few tears.'

Dens fans will never know the extent of Duffy's devastation but I doubt if they will ever forget the moment the sad news was broken on the radio after a match at Cappielow. Ours was not the only car-load struck dumb by the tragic news.

'I think it really affected the players as well. I got on great with them — I have an awful lot of friends at the club — and I think they felt for me because they all knew what football meant to me and how much I would miss it.'

The club tried their best to keep Duffy involved training the young players but his eye would wander to where the first team men were.

Jim Duffy had touched every one involved with the club — not just the fans — and it must have been tough, too, for all who work with the club, as the realisation dawned that his days as a player were over.

Team-mate George McGeachie's generosity in offering Duffy his own testimonial match against Liverpool was typical of the kindness shown. 'It was fantastic, what the club, players and supporters did for me. It was great to have that feeling of friendship and appreciation — it was phenomenal. I couldn't really speak to the supporters at the dinner because of the lump im my throat. I just couldn't put into words what it all meant to me.'

Duffy was touched too, by the readiness and willingness shown by his peers to play for a Scotland Select against Dundee in his testimonial. Phone calls from big-names who couldn't make it, a match fee donation from top referee David Syme . . . all these things helped make it a very special memory. But none of that compared to the warmth and feeling that glowed from the South Enclosure that December afternoon as the Dens choir sang their own tear-touched tribute — 'One Jim Duffy, there's only one Jim Duffy.' When he came over to salute them, you got the impression Duffy wanted to jump the wall and shake each and every one by the hand. They'd have waited all night to get their turn.

That close-season after steering the Dundee youth team to

Man in the middle . . . Somewhere in this lot is Albert Kidd who has just scored against Hearts on the day Dundee shattered the Gorgie title dream.

the BP Cup Final, Duffy parted company with the club. 'It wasn't until I had actually moved from the area that I was able to put the club to the back of my mind and try to get on with the rest of my life.'

At that stage Duffy thought his future lay with the public house he'd bought in Glasgow but football hadn't forgotten him. Out of the blue he got a call from Gordon McQueen and he started as assistant manager at Airdrie.

He'd hardly got the seat warm before he was at Brockville as Britain's youngest manager at the ripe old age of 29.

'I couldn't believe it. I'd only recently left the game, was an assistant for only a few weeks and then I was a manager in my own right and with an ambitious club like Falkirk.

'I got an unbelievable response from the Falkirk support and we had a good season although we were pipped by Dunfermline for promotion. We managed to turn things around and changed the idea people had of the club from being a defensive-minded outfit that seemed to want only to survive into an attacking, footballing side.'

Duffy quit the job early in his second season 'definitely an error on my part — the way I handled it'. An error may be, but it gave Duffy the chance to think about playing again. Encouraged by his old Possil YM pal Tony Fitzpatrick, he began training at Love Street and the burning desire looked as if it might reach fruition.

Dundee had first option and once several red tape and financial hurdles had been cleared Duffy was back at Dens.

His first top-team game was in the Forfarshire Cup Final at McDiarmid Park when both Dundee and St Johnstone were out of the Scottish Cup and otherwise idle.

'Rab Shannon was captain and I collided with him right at the start and he had to go off. When we won the Cup they made me captain in his place so there I was, my first competitive game back and I was holding aloft a trophy.'

Duffy is a one-off, he takes his football as seriously as the next man, but likes a bit of fun. A respected coach said to him in exasperation — 'When are you going to grow up?' He was referring to the man who once spoiled a Falkirk team group photograph by wearing a gorilla mask, the joker who with fellow teetotaller Tosh McKinlay could play the best drunks in town when the players were on a night out, and the coach who took a Partick Thistle training session wearing a 'Biggles' hat 'to set me apart so the players could tell who was meant to be doing the coaching.'

But, sadly, there was nothing funny about his departure from Dens Park. 'When I re-joined Dundee, I sold my pub in Glasgow because I thought I'd be signing for Dundee on a long-term basis. I had no other aim than to play for Dundee.

'I felt I had proved to the club I was fit enough to play again and felt they were really sort of asking me to do it all over again. I needed stability, whether it was length of contract or some sort of player-coach role like the one I now have at Partick. But obviously, I didn't want to see anyone out of a job, the club was in the First Division and cutting costs and really that was not an option — that was no-one's fault, it just wasn't an option, it was as simple as that.

'I was happy to come to some arrangement whereby if I played so many games I would get so much money. As it wore on, we would get close, then drift away. Anyone who knew me knew how much I wanted to play for Dundee but when I'd signed the contract in the first place I had an agreement that if things didn't work out I could move on and they'd be repaid what they'd laid out insurance wise. But Gordon Wallace had a different interpretation and we've since spoken about it and agreed to differ.

'I've made a couple of big mistakes in football, the first being my departure from Falkirk and the second the way I handled the Dundee thing. Probably my nature made me a bit rash in both instances and possibly I was maybe more intent on getting my own back on some statements from individuals that had come out of the club. Instead, I should have thanked the supporters for giving me the opportunity to get back into the playing side explaining that, all things considered it was better for me and my family to stay in Glasgow and have job security. I think most people would have accepted that.

'I have loved the club from the moment Archie Knox signed me and I still do. My son Paul still supports Dundee — he's the only Dundee supporter at his school — and my daughter Kim was born in the city. So you will understand that these things add to the affection I have for the club and for the city and that will never leave me.'

Likewise, the memory of Jim Duffy in a Dundee jersey will never leave all who saw him.